Praise for

HOW ALEXANDER HAMILTON SCREWED UP AMERICA

"A thinking American must choose between Hamilton and Jefferson, whose contrary visions of the future were contested in the first days of the Constitution. If you are happy with big government, big banks, big business, big military, and judicial dictatorship, then you have Hamilton to thank. His legacy of nationalism, centralization, crony capitalism, and military adventurism is all around us. If you prefer the Jeffersonian version of an American regime (or even if you don't) McClanahan's new book is for you. This is not simply a polemic. McClanahan, who is proving to be one of the ablest truly *relevant* historians of our time, has given us a definitive, deeply-researched chapter and verse and long perspective of who this bad man was and how he is the fountain of our current discontents."

> —CLYDE WILSON, professor of history, emeritus, University of South Carolina

"Brion McClanahan masterfully shows that we live today in Alexander Hamilton's dream of America—and this is our chief ailment. The national debt, militaristic foreign policy, and expansive powers for the national government can all be traced to the mind and work of Hamilton. But this book is more than just an indictment of the Hamiltonian program. McClanahan points to a forgotten legacy of decentralization and the beauty of small and vibrant self-governing communities. He challenges us to rediscover First Principles championed by Thomas Jefferson, John Taylor of Caroline, and St. George Tucker. In a time of growing nationalism, this book is a must read for every thinking American."

> —WILLIAM J. WATKINS, JR., author of *Crossroads for Liberty: Recovering the Anti-Federalist Values of America's First Constitution*

"Lin-Manuel Miranda's *Hamilton* plays up the heroic angle, essentially ignoring its subject's misdeeds. Brion McClanahan gets straight to the meat of the matter: Alexander Hamilton's destructive constitutional legacy. It is not a pretty picture. McClanahan shows that Hamilton's contemporaries realized what his impact would be at the time, and then provides a forceful account of Hamiltonianism's effects from the Founders' day to ours. This is essential reading."

—KEVIN GUTZMAN, American constitutional scholar and historian and professor of history at Western Connecticut State University

"*How Alexander Hamilton Screwed Up America* is a must-read book for anyone who wants to know how the American rule of law was transformed into rule by leftist lawyers determined to ignore or destroy all constitutional limits on governmental powers. It was Hamilton and his main disciples, Justices Story, Marshall, and Black, who betrayed the principles of the American founding with such fantasies as 'implied powers' of the Constitution. This paved the way for the modern welfare/warfare state which 'would not exist without Hamilton's machinations,' writes McClanahan. This is the real reason why Alexander Hamilton is the 'new hero for the left.' McClanahan exposes Hamilton's lies, deceptions, and Machiavellian plots to paint a vivid picture of the real Alexander Hamilton."

—DR. THOMAS DILORENZO, professor of economics, Loyola University Maryland, and author of *Hamilton's Curse: How Jefferson's Arch Enemy Betrayed the American Revolution— and What It Means for Americans Today*

"Brion McClanahan is that rarity: an historian who tells the truth. Read his exposé of the bird on the ten-dollar bill. Not only will you learn a lot the establishment doesn't want you to know, you'll have fun doing it."

—LEW ROCKWELL, founder and chairman of the Ludwig von Mises Institute

"Today, we live under crushing taxes and debt. And the central government intrudes into nearly every aspect of society, from defining marriage to policing the length of high school students' hair. This was not a revolution where the people amended the Constitution. It was a revolution by members of the central government against the Constitution. How was this possible? Brion McClanahan shows how Alexander Hamilton (who described the Constitution as a 'frail and worthless fabric') created a strategy—later followed by others—that enabled the central government to become a self-centralizing machine."

    —DONALD W. LIVINGSTON, professor of philosophy, emeritus, Emory University

"Here's a rule that will serve you well: whenever a political figure is beloved of all sides, he's always a scoundrel. Brion McClanahan rips the benign mask off Alexander Hamilton, who is presented in American classrooms as a great hero to celebrate. He is, as Brion shows, one of the original villains in the American story. Set a match to your seventh-grade textbook, and get the real story from *How Alexander Hamilton Screwed Up America*."

    —TOM WOODS, *New York Times* bestselling author and host of *The Tom Woods Show*

HOW ALEXANDER HAMILTON SCREWED UP AMERICA

HOW ALEXANDER HAMILTON SCREWED UP AMERICA

BRION McCLANAHAN

REGNERY
HISTORY

Regnery History™ is a trademark of Salem Communications Holding Corporation; Regnery® is a registered trademark of Salem Communications Holding Corporation

ISBN 978-1-62157-635-8
First e-book edition 2017: 978-1-62157-654-9

Cataloging-in-Publication Data on file with the Library of Congress

Published in the United States by
Regnery History
An imprint of Regnery Publishing
A Division of Salem Media Group
300 New Jersey Ave NW
Washington, DC 20001
www.RegneryHistory.com

Manufactured in the United States of America

10 9 8 7 6 5 4 3 2 1

Books are available in quantity for promotional or premium use. For information on discounts and terms, please visit our website: www.Regnery.com.

Distributed to the trade by
Perseus Distribution
www.perseusdistribution.com

To Tim McClanahan 1970–2016

CONTENTS

FOREWORD

RON PAUL

The central government has always been the greatest threat to liberty in America, but most Americans don't understand how modern America became the warfare state. How did the president acquire so much unconstitutional power? How did the federal judiciary become, at times, the most powerful branch of government? How were the states reduced to mere corporations of the general government? Why is every issue, from abortion to bathrooms to crime to education, a "national" problem? The people have very little input into public policy. They vote, they rally, they attend "town hall" meetings, but it does very little to stop the avalanche of federal laws, regulations, and rules that affect every aspect of American life. We have a federal leviathan that can't be tamed, and Americans are angry about it. They want answers.

Certainly, the Framers of the Constitution did not design our system this way. They intended the checks and balances between the three branches of government and also between the states and the central government to limit the potential for abuse, but somewhere along the way that changed. Who or what changed the system? It wasn't Barack Obama or George W. Bush. It wasn't even Franklin Roosevelt, his cousin Teddy, or Woodrow Wilson. They certainly helped, but as Brion McClanahan argues in the following pages, the architects of our nationalist nightmare were none other than Alexander Hamilton and a trio of Supreme Court justices: John Marshall, Joseph Story, and Hugo Black. Identifying the source of the problem is essential for correcting it.

Hamilton has become one of the more popular figures in America for the Left and the Right, so accusing him of making a mess of the United States is certainly shocking. But it is also accurate. Hamilton's constitutional machinations created the outline for literally every unconstitutional federal act, from executive and judicial overreach to the nationalization of every political issue in the country. He lied to the American public about his true intentions before the Constitution was ratified and then used sly doublespeak to persuade others that so-called "implied powers" were part of the plan from the beginning. We would not have abusive unilateral executive authority in foreign and domestic policy, dangerous central banking, and impotent state governments without Hamilton's guidance. Hamilton is the architect of big government in America.

Marshall, Story, and Black certainly acted as co-conspirators. Marshall's landmark decisions could have been written by Hamilton. His reading of the Constitution was at odds with how the document was explained to the state ratifying conventions in 1788. Marshall's interpretation would have led the people to reject the document. His belief in federal judicial supremacy and unchecked national authority has been the keystone to every subsequent outrageous federal ruling, from *Roe v. Wade* to *NIFB v. Sebelius*. Marshall is the reason the Supreme Court now takes center stage in every political debate in America, but he did not accomplish this alone.

Marshall's protégé and right hand man Joseph Story codified Marshall's vision for federal judicial supremacy as a popular legal scholar and law professor. Even today, law students across the country are taught

Story's version of federal power. Story's message is simple: the federal government is supreme (even if it isn't), the state governments are subservient to the central authority, and the federal court system is the final arbiter in all constitutional questions. When these law students become lawyers and judges, they echo Story's teachings. With a legal profession so infested with a version of American political history contradictory to the actual record, it is no wonder the federal judiciary has become a mere rubber stamp in the expansion of federal power.

Black put the finishing touches on the Hamiltonian coup. As a member of the Supreme Court in the mid-twentieth century, Black participated in the final transformation of America from a federal union that respected state powers to a unitary state with unlimited control over the lives of individual Americans. You can't pray in public schools, control who uses public bathrooms, regulate pornography, or keep common standards of public decency because of Hugo Black. His insistence that the majority of the people of the states had very little influence over the social standards of their own communities delivered a death blow to the original Constitution. Thanks to Black, Americans now believe every issue is national, no matter how local in scope.

McClanahan has done a service to those who love liberty and respect the original Constitution as drafted and ratified by the founding generation. By knowing how we went wrong and who drove America off the rails, Americans can begin to repair the damage done to our political system. Unrestrained nationalism is a curse, but there is an antidote: liberty and federalism. If we start to cultivate liberty and freedom in our own communities and insist that our elected officials pursue the same agenda by disengaging the general government from Hamilton's desire for unchecked national power, we could salvage real America from the ruins of Hamilton's America. Education is the first step, and reading this book is a nice place to start.

INTRODUCTION

On the evening of November 19, 2016, Vice President-elect Mike Pence attended a performance of the Broadway musical *Hamilton*. After the curtain call, Pence prepared to leave as the actors took their bows, but Brandon Victor Dixon—who plays Vice President Aaron Burr in the show—asked the audience to wait while he read a prepared statement to Pence and encouraged everyone in attendance to take out their phones, record, Tweet, and post the moment. Many complied and some even booed Pence, among them leftist singer Bob Geldof, a man unhappy with the "Brexit" vote and the rise of conservative "populism" in the world.[1]

Dixon thanked Pence for attending, then read his political diatribe: "We, sir, are the diverse America who are alarmed and anxious that your new administration will not protect us, our planet, our children, our parents, or defend us and uphold our inalienable rights, sir. But we truly hope that this show has inspired you to uphold our American values and to work on behalf of all of us. All of us. Again, we truly thank you for sharing this show, this wonderful American story told by a diverse group of men, women of different colors, creeds, and orientations." The cast nodded in agreement and most of the audience cheered. They had already booed and heckled Pence several times before and during the show.[2] President-elect Donald Trump took to Twitter and blasted Dixon, calling his actions "unfair" and demanding an apology.

While childish, this episode is indicative of a larger political and historical problem. Alexander Hamilton, it seems, has been reinvented by Lin-Manuel Miranda. He is the new hero for the Left, a hipster who personified the immigrant experience, pursued active central government, and championed the notion of a "diverse" America. The alt-Left website *Vox* recently called the remixed music of the show the soundtrack for a new revolution.[3] All he needs is a man-bun and shaggy beard. But is this true? Somewhat. Hamilton had for most of American history been the darling of the *right*. The assumption that he would have supported either Dixon's antics or the modern leftist agenda would have been thought laughable until recently. Hamilton was no "man of the people," but he was the architect of modern "big government" in America. He didn't see it that way, but the modern welfare/warfare state would not exist without Hamilton's constitutional machinations. Hamilton gave us guns and butter.

It would also be unfair, however, to lay the entire burden of unconstitutional government at Hamilton's feet. He had help, particularly from the United States Supreme Court. What Hamilton could not accomplish during his brief time in American government, the Supreme Court solidified over the next 160 years. The homespun John Marshall, the "constitutional scholar" Joseph Story, and the "populist" Hugo Black completed Hamilton's nationalist vision. They were complicit participants in distorting the American founding.

The title of this book is intended to be shocking. How could a man so celebrated by both the Left and the Right, a member of the glorious founding generation, a generation I have called the greatest in American history, be responsible for "screwing up America?"[4] And what about Marshall and Story? Both men are celebrated jurists, with Marshall considered perhaps the most important federal judge in the history of America. Story's *Commentaries on the Constitution* is still studied in law schools across the country. The progressive Black, though his opinions on the Fourteenth Amendment are often celebrated by libertarians, is a more obvious choice for modern conservatives as one who might have "screwed things up." Every time an American suggests he or she has a "constitutional right" to keep and bear arms, for example, Black should get the credit. He did more to create the illusion that the Bill of Rights protects Americans from both federal *and* state law than anyone else in history, but this is a perversion of the original Constitution and a major culprit in the establishment of the insane modern leftist legal world.

And we can't escape any of these men. For example, in the controversial *National Federation of Independent Business v. Sebelius* (2012), better known as the decision that upheld the constitutionality of "Obamacare," Chief Justice John Roberts cited the case *Hylton v. United States* (1791) in support of his belief that "Obamacare," as a tax, was constitutional.[5] This was Hamilton speaking from the grave. He represented the United States before the Supreme Court in this case and outlined a broad interpretation of congressional taxing power. "Obamacare" could also be called "Hamiltoncare." Don't agree with same-sex "marriage"? Thank Hamilton and Black. Opposed to government-imposed "transgender bathrooms"? Again, Hamilton and the decisions of Marshall and Story are the root of the problem. Don't like the welfare state? Hamilton is the culprit. Object to the "pornification" of America? Black's fingerprints are all over it. Our "national" focus on such vital issues as education, healthcare, the environment, labor laws, marriage, etc. is the byproduct of two hundred years of Hamiltonian conditioning codified by several important Supreme Court decisions. As a result, we tend to view the states as the enemies of "progress," the burr under the saddle on the rump of "good" and "efficient" government. Americans need to unlearn that lesson.

To be blunt, Hamilton's "American nation" is little more than a fraud. Step by step, Hamilton refocused the way even men of his own generation thought about the central government. He sold them a bill of goods during ratification and then pulled the rug out from under them once in power. His arguments in favor of "loose construction" forged the constitutional underpinnings of every Supreme Court decision that upheld his agenda, both during the Marshall Court and into the twenty-first century. To be fair, none of these men were *always* wrong. All four were generally decent men of their time (Hamilton and Black had their moral failings), and all firmly believed that national centralization would protect and secure American liberty. But history has shown that each built his case on quicksand. The United States Constitution was never intended to be interpreted the way Hamilton, Marshall, Story, and Black insisted it was during their political and legal careers. The evidence is all against them.

If Americans want to rekindle what "made America great" they should recognize American nationalism for what it is, a house of cards built on false premises and imaginative construction. Doing so, however, requires that Americans realize that Hamilton, Marshall, Story, and Black screwed up America. This may not be an easy pill to swallow, but it would go a long way toward restoring the original intent of the Constitution and real federalism in America.

CHAPTER ONE

HAMILTON VS. HAMILTON

Alexander Hamilton is one of the three most important members of the founding generation, and it could be argued that he is *the* most important member. His reputation has been revitalized since the 1990s, most conspicuously by Ron Chernow's runaway best-selling biography and later by Miranda's Broadway hit musical *Hamilton*, but it was not always so stellar. Hamilton was at one time the punching bag for the anti-elitist strain of the progressive Left, many of whom considered the American founders to be little more than self-interested, racist aristocrats without concern for the "common man." Never mind that the much respected progressive philosopher Herbert Croly called for a federal government that mixed the activism of Hamilton with the democracy of Thomas Jefferson to create a real "progressive" agenda. Hamilton's ideas on federal power were as much a part of the Square Deal and the New Deal as Jeffersonian appeals to the common man.

Even while denigrating the Founding Fathers in general, most leftist Americans viewed Jefferson as one of their own, the people's president who favored the laboring class over the well-heeled members of an old American aristocratic order. Hamilton then took the role of villain, the greedy capitalist lining up with American big business and special interests, the true architect of the ruinous American economic order that favored profits over people, money over man. This false narrative influenced generations of Americans, even those on the Right, who began to see Hamilton and the Federalists as their intellectual forefathers. If the Left admired Jefferson, then the Right had to not only accept Hamilton, but embrace him.

And there was much to like. Hamilton, more than any other member of the founding generation, represented the real "American ideal." He was born a bastard son in the British West Indies, a young boy who pulled himself up by his bootstraps after his father abandoned him and his mother died. When he was just a teenager he was allowed to run a thriving merchant firm in the West Indies while the proprietor was away on business. Hamilton arrived in America in 1772, and during the crisis with Great Britain he caught the eye of several leading patriots with the publication of two political writings that showed both maturity and guile. This would become a hallmark of his career. If nothing else, Hamilton was a skilled writer and rhetorician with a persuasive and elegant pen. But this is not how Hamilton wanted to be remembered. Like many young men filled with martial vigor, Hamilton wanted glory on the battlefield.

He volunteered for service during the early stages of the American War for Independence. Hamilton could never be called a "sunshine patriot." He stood firmly with independence from the outset of hostilities and maintained his resolve even through the darkest periods of the war. Much of that time was spent as George Washington's aide-de-camp. Appointed to that position at only twenty-one, Hamilton had access to both the leading men in America and foreign leaders, particularly the Marquis de Lafayette of France. Washington recognized Hamilton's talents, and the close relationship between the two would later help mold and define the powers of the general government. Hamilton was aspiring, hard working, intelligent, and determined. What he lacked in proper rearing he made up for in observation and ambition, and he loved America, so much so he was willing to die for it during the war.

And here is an important distinction. Hamilton never claimed a state as his home. He settled in New York and married into the Schuyler family, one of the oldest and wealthiest clans in the state, but his attachment was to *America* and not New York. This American nationalism represented a key difference between Hamilton and Jefferson. Jefferson called Virginia his country and had a commitment to federalism based on provincial attachment to his native soil. To Jefferson, not all issues were national, and not all issues were worthy of discussion in the federal capital. Yet, to Hamilton, preservation of a strong central government became an essential component in an effort to root out dangerous forms of democratic thought, and arrest a potential slide into an American version of the French Revolution. His exemplar was the British Constitution and the old European order, an order Hamilton was not born into but adopted by custom and practice. Russell Kirk doted on Hamilton in his famous *The Conservative Mind*, but he thought Hamilton was too idealistic to understand how a strong central government could undermine his efforts to eradicate the leveling spirit of the eighteenth century. Kirk was just another in a long line of intellectual historians who passed Hamilton over in favor of other Founders to cherish. The longtime conservative historian Forrest McDonald discussed Hamilton's financial brilliance in a 1979 biography, but it was little noticed outside of academic circles.[1] Hamilton's reputation waited patiently to be rescued from the intellectual abyss of the progressive era.

That all changed in 1992 when the conservative columnist George Will wrote that, "There is an elegant memorial in Washington to Jefferson, but none to Hamilton. However, if you seek Hamilton's monument, look around. You are living in it. We honor Jefferson, but live in Hamilton's country, a mighty industrial nation with a strong central government."[2] Five years later, conservative commentators David Brooks and William Kristol penned a clever op-ed in the *Wall Street Journal* aimed at making Hamilton the poster boy for modern conservatism. Both argued the nationalism of Hamilton should be emulated in order to establish what they called a "national greatness conservatism."[3] In 1999, *National Review* editor Richard Brookhiser published a highly laudatory biography of Hamilton that attempted to resurrect Hamilton's reputation as a financial wizard, making the same claims McDonald had in 1979.[4] The American capitalist economy, they argued, owed its success to Hamilton. The New York Historical Society made Brookhiser's book the centerpiece of a traveling exhibition on Hamilton, and just five years later, Ron Chernow's thick biography of the first secretary of the treasury rocketed to the top of the *New York Times* bestseller list. While Chernow is no conservative, his treatment of Hamilton resonated with every conservative thinker who adopted Hamilton as "their guy." To these conservatives, Hamilton represented what was best about America, namely big business, big banks, and a big military.

But if conservatives now believed that Hamilton was *the* man to emulate, they soon had to fight the progressive Left for that honor. It seems all the attention Hamilton was receiving led the Left to rethink their disdain for the man. Maybe he was one of *them*. In 1997, leftist historian Michael Lind's *Hamilton's Republic* traced Hamilton's influence from Lincoln to LBJ.[5] It seems Hamilton was pretty good after all. Who could deny the expansion of the general government in the twentieth century to fight poverty, racism, and injustice? Wasn't that "Hamilton's Republic"?

Others soon echoed that sentiment. In 2002, liberal political scientist Stephen Knott published an intellectual biography which claimed that all of the great accomplishments of the twentieth century, from beating back fascism in World War II, to space exploration, to open borders, and the eradication of Jim Crow segregation, were all directly attributable to "Hamilton's America."[6] Liberals began worshipping Hamilton so much that the leftist Brookings Institute dusted off "The Hamilton Project" in 2006, a program aimed at creating more government influence in social programs. All of this landed Hamilton on Broadway via a hip-hop tour through the founding generation that champions his immigrant past, his rags to riches story, and his influential pen. To the producers of the show, *that* Hamilton, though flawed, embodies the American spirit. Barack Obama has called the show, and by default Hamilton's life, a "story for all of us and about all of us."

So who is the real Alexander Hamilton? The elitist champion of finance capitalism and "national greatness conservatism" or the social justice warrior who drew up the blueprints for every progressive program of the twentieth century?

At least to an extent, both, and therein lies the problem with Hamilton worship.

Hamilton spoke out of both sides of his mouth. Put simply, he often lied, particularly when it came to defending federal power. Hamilton would craft a narrative of constitutional authority that would fit his agenda, but that narrative was often at odds with the story he spun when the Constitution was in the process of ratification. In 1787 and 1788, Hamilton sang a tune of federal restraint and limited central authority. When backed into a corner by Jefferson or James Madison after the Constitution was ratified, Hamilton would often backtrack and advance positions he favored during the Philadelphia Convention, namely for a supreme central authority with virtually unlimited power, particularly for the executive branch. This Hamilton was the real Hamilton, but the real Hamilton would never have been in a position to direct the future of the United States had he not been part of a disingenuous sales pitch to the states while the Constitution was being debated and ratified.

In 1811, Jefferson retold a story of a dinner party he once hosted, attended by both Hamilton and John Adams during George Washington's first term in office. Washington asked Jefferson to arrange the gathering, and as they were sitting around the table enjoying their wine, the conversation turned to the merits and defects of the British Constitution. Jefferson said that Adams argued, "if some of its defects and abuses were corrected, it would be the most perfect constitution of government ever devised by man." Hamilton rejoined that, "with its existing vices, it was the most perfect model of government that could be formed; and that the correction of its vices would render it an impracticable government." A bit later,

Hamilton's attention turned to several portraits hanging around the room. He asked Jefferson who they were, and Jefferson responded that they were his "trinity of the three greatest men the world had ever produced," namely Sir Francis Bacon, Sir Isaac Newton, and John Locke. Hamilton gave a long pause, and responded "that the greatest man who ever lived was Julius Caesar." Jefferson explained that this statement offered the clearest window into Hamilton's political philosophy. "Hamilton [was] honest as a man, but, as a politician, believing in the necessity of either force or corruption to govern men."[7]

The claim of his being "honest as a man" is debatable. Hamilton had a lengthy affair with a married woman, and even after he was threatened with blackmail continued to carry on the dalliance by paying for her "services," all while his wife was ill. He engaged in clandestine diplomacy with the British while claiming to favor neutrality to both Washington and Jefferson. He openly lied to both men about his activities. He obtained a battlefield commission without Washington's knowledge or approval during the American War for Independence and then blasted Washington's character in several private letters. Washington never knew of Hamilton's duplicity and always treated him like a son.

But Jefferson was certainly correct in his assessment of Hamilton's political character. He was a consistent advocate of national supremacy in the 1790s, even if that required "force or corruption," and he would lie to advance his grand vision of "everlasting glory" as the historian M. E. Bradford called it. But we should listen to the Hamilton of the *Federalist* essays and the Hamilton who defended the Constitution at the New York Ratifying Convention in 1788, even if that Hamilton was at odds with Hamilton as secretary of the treasury. This gives us a more complete picture of the man. He was more than a bastard immigrant who found "everlasting glory" in America and who laid the foundation for American finance capital, corporate welfare, and progressive social programs. Hamilton was a duplicitous man whose personality and ambition led to an America and a Constitution at odds with the one he publicly supported in 1788 and that the American public bought as a result.

That is the real story of Alexander Hamilton. Despite his gift for rhetoric and high reputation as a Founding Father, he was simply not to be trusted, neither then nor now.

CHAPTER TWO

FROM PHILADELPHIA TO POUGHKEEPSIE

June 28, 1788. The New York Ratifying Convention in Pough-keepsie had reached its eleventh day, and the tempers of the delegates exceeded the heat and humidity outside. Though ratification of the Constitution was certain by this date (ten states had already ratified), when the Convention began on June 17, it appeared that New York would be the deciding state in the creation of a new central government. This put tremendous pressure on the proponents of the document. They had to move men, or the Constitution would potentially be a dead letter. Hamilton, along with fellow New Yorker John Jay and Virginian James Madison, had already spent months arguing for the Constitution as Publius in the now famous—though hardly influential at the time—*Federalist* essays. If New York did not ratify, Hamilton's efforts would have been in vain.

A vote against ratification would place the state in a precarious position. If the opponents of the document had their way, the Empire State would retain its position as a "free and independent state" and avoid the perceived pitfalls of a stronger central government, but this would make it impossible for the state to be considered for the home of the new federal capital. Hamilton and his federalist comrades had to convince the Convention that New York would be safe within the Union, and to do that, they had to ensure these wavering delegates that the states would retain all powers not expressly granted to the general government by the Constitution. This was no easy sell.

For several days, three powerful voices against ratification—George Clinton, Melancton Smith, and John Lansing—had verbally pounded the expanded powers of the new central authority. Lansing and Smith carried much of the debate for the opposition to the Constitution at Poughkeepsie. Clinton was the sitting governor of New York. His broad shoulders, wide girth, and large nose were matched only by the substantial patronage and political clout he wielded. When Madison wrote in *Federalist* No. 10 that the Constitution would limit the influence of factions, it was men like Clinton, Patrick Henry, and John Hancock that he had in mind. This triumvirate of dominant state leaders worried those who favored the Constitution. Their perceived fiefdoms were seen as detrimental to concerted action, particularly during military or economic emergencies. Henry and Hancock had already been tamed in Virginia and Massachusetts respectively, but Clinton was not going down without a fight. He was a hard-nosed Irish brawler, a veteran of both the French and Indian War and the American War for Independence, and a political knee capper who protected his friends and destroyed his enemies. As governor, Clinton had used far-reaching confiscation powers to strip former Tories of their lands in order to keep state taxes to a minimum.

Even before the convention met in June, Clinton had been waging a war of the pen against the document. Writing as Cato on October 25, 1787, Clinton asked if the "inhabitants of Georgia, or New Hampshire, will have the same obligations towards you as your own, and preside over your lives, liberties, and property, with the same care and attachment?" He answered his rhetorical question in the negative and insisted that "the strongest principle of union resides within our domestic walls."[1] Clinton then refused to call a convention in an attempt to block ratification. This may have been a mistake, for if New York had met before Massachusetts or Virginia, it might have set the tone and led to an "anti-federalist" victory. Regardless, his speeches at Poughkeepsie maintained a familiar theme: the Constitution would subvert the lives, liberty, and property of the people of New York and reduce the state to a mere province within an uncontrollable centralized regime.

Smith was of a different breed but no less fiery than Governor Clinton. A wealthy and powerful merchant who had made a name for himself as a zealous patriot during the American War for Independence, Smith's impassioned cries against the proposed Constitution were those of an idealist. He had neither the political strength of Clinton nor the influence outside of his home district (where it was considerable), but his speeches against ratification were nevertheless persuasive and helped serve as the backbone of the opposition. When Smith finally buckled under the realization that ratification was a foregone conclusion and threw his conditional support behind the proposed document after proponents promised it could be amended, Clinton considered it the fatal blow for the opposition.

Smith opined early in the ratification convention that "the intent of the Constitution was not a confederacy, but a reduction of all the states into a consolidated government...." and considered the "abolition of the *state constitutions* as an event fatal to the liberties of America.... In a country where a portion of the people lives more than twelve hundred miles from the centre, I think that one body cannot possibly legislate for the whole." The Constitution, Smith said, would establish a government that would be free to fleece the people and "command...our persons." This was due to the destruction of the real federalism embodied by the Articles of Confederation. "A few years ago, we fought for liberty; we framed a general government on free principles; we placed the state legislatures, in whom the people have a full and a fair representation, between Congress and the people...."[2]

Lansing was perhaps the most formidable opponent of the three. He was polished, well-educated, and perhaps the wealthiest man in New York, a gentleman's gentleman. Whereas Clinton preferred a fist-fight and Smith a knifing rejoinder, Lansing's speeches exhibited refinement and craft. He engaged his opponents with wit and disinterested determination. After all, as a man with a large Hudson River estate and a family history that dated to the earliest Dutch settlers in the area, Lansing had no need to prove himself. Unlike Clinton and Smith, or for that matter Hamilton, Lansing was a product of an older established order. His story was not one of ambition and "rags to riches," but one of tradition. His speeches reflected this during the ratification convention.

Lansing feared that the innovations of the new Constitution would destroy the states and render them impotent in opposition to tyranny. He said as much during his single speech at the Philadelphia Convention on June 16, 1787, arguing that "New York would never have concurred in sending deputies to the Convention, if she had supposed the deliberations were to turn on a consolidation of the states, and a national government."[3] Now, a year later, he was faced with a Constitution that in his mind did just that. As a result, he favored an amendment that would have allowed New York to secede if their proposals for a bill of rights were not accepted in a timely manner. That motion was defeated, but it showed Lansing's commitment to individual liberty and the original federal republic.

Hamilton had made clear his support for the Constitution before the Poughkeepsie convention, though no one knew for certain in June 1788 that Hamilton was the primary author of the *Federalist* essays. There were whispers it was true, and opponents of the document had called him out in Poughkeepsie for the obvious similarities between the arguments put forth in those essays and Hamilton's choice of words in attempting to persuade the Convention that the Constitution was necessary. He denied being involved, but Hamilton made a habit of lying when the need arose. Additionally, opponents of the document had a hard time trusting that Hamilton actually meant what he said, particularly those who knew his positions on the Articles of Confederation and the need for greater central authority, including the elimination of the states.

That much was evident at the Philadelphia Convention. On June 18, 1787, Hamilton gave one of the more controversial speeches of the proceedings. The historian Forrest McDonald claimed it raised the tone of the Convention and "repolarized the debates," although as McDonald also points out it "scarcely turned the convention around." William Samuel Johnson of Connecticut said a few days later that Hamilton's speech had been "praised by everybody" but was "supported by none."[4]

Hamilton's speech was certainly innovative, and it marked the only substantial comments Hamilton made during the Convention, comments that he later tried to run from (unsuccessfully) at Poughkeepsie. Hamilton opened his speech by declaring his opposition to both the so-called Virginia Plan and the New Jersey Plan. Defects, he said, could be found in both. The major problem, as Hamilton saw it, was in trying to maintain the federal nature of the general government, meaning a union of sovereign states. This was not only impracticable but idiotic because what America needed, in Hamilton's opinion, was a truly national government. This would eliminate the several obvious problems in the federal republic under the Articles of Confederation.

According to Hamilton, these problems could be boiled down to five. One, the states had no interest in supporting the general government because "they constantly pursue internal interests adverse to those of the whole." Two, the "love of power" allowed for both the elevation of demagogues to positions of importance in the state governments and the increasing importance of the state vis-à-vis the general government. "Consider," said Hamilton, "what such a state as Virginia will be in a few years—a few compared with the life of nations. How strongly will it feel its importance and self-sufficiency!" Three, Hamilton believed that the people of the states were too attached to their state governments and would side with them over the interests of the whole. Four, because of this attachment, military force would be unable to coerce the states into compliance. Force was necessary, Hamilton opined, "over large communities," but not possible in a federal republic. The end result would be a "dissolution of the Union." Fifth, Hamilton concluded that because of the nature of the current Union, meaning the supremacy of the states, "all the passions…of avarice, ambition, interest, which govern most individuals, and all public bodies, fall into the current of the states, and do not flow in the stream of the general government. The former, therefore, will generally be an overmatch for the general government, and render any confederacy in its very nature precarious."

Hamilton then proposed the solution to this problem: jettison the states and create a national government. Why? Because "all of the weight of [government] is on the side of the states; and must continue so long as the states continue to exist," and Hamilton thought "that great economy might be obtained by substituting a general government" for the current system. His plan for a new national government included a senate and a president elected for life without any check on their legislative or executive authority, a "supreme judicial authority" with appellate jurisdiction over all laws, both state (which he reduced to "corporations") and national, and a "supremacy clause" that would void "all laws of the particular states contrary to the constitution or laws of the United States." And to ensure that the states would be unable to pass such laws, Hamilton further advocated that the governor of each state "be appointed by the general government, and shall have a negative upon the laws about to be passed in the state of which he is governor or president." Hamilton then suggested that the militia be placed under the "exclusive direction of the United States," meaning the states would have no recourse in opposing abuse by the "national" government.

This proposal would be shocking, but "he saw no *other* necessity for declining it." Hamilton knew that the delegates to the Philadelphia Convention and the people of the states at large would not support such a move out of sheer "shock," but if they rationally considered the situation, they would realize only a national government without the encumbrance of the states could be relied upon to deliver the type of efficient government he and other nationalists desired. He pithily remarked that simply modifying the current form of popular government would be *"but pork still, with a little change of sauce."* The states, Hamilton declared, were "not necessary for any of the great purposes of commerce, revenue, or agriculture." Hamilton recognized that "subordinate authorities...would be necessary," but he called them "corporations for local purposes." This reduction of the states to mere "corporations for local purposes" and his version of the "supremacy clause" were constitutional machinations that had lasting effects and would rear their ugly heads later in American history, but at that time, Hamilton knew they would never be accepted.[5] They were, in fact, rejected outright by the Philadelphia Convention. Hamilton understood that he was not arguing for "his" Constitution when he began penning the *Federalist* essays in the fall of 1787.

Hamilton took up the issue of federal supremacy and conflict over the powers and ultimate necessity of the states on two important occasions: first in *Federalist* No. 32 and 33 on January 2, 1788, and second in the June 27 speech in Poughkeepsie that brought the convention to a standstill. *Federalist* No. 32 and 33 outlined several of the arguments James Madison would make in the more famous *Federalist* No. 45, but Hamilton was responding to the "virulent invective and petulant declamation against the proposed Constitution," the aim of which was to create a "misrepresentation" of the proposed lawmaking powers of the general government "as the pernicious engines by which their local governments were to be destroyed and their liberties exterminated...." Hamilton, like the other proponents of the Constitution, recognized that the key sticking point for those opposed to the Constitution was the potential elimination or reduction of the states. He had advocated this very position in Philadelphia, but his plan was rejected, and so Hamilton had to persuade the wavering masses that the states would be secure and that the new general government could not exceed its delegated authority by infringing on the reserved powers of the states. Because no one knew who wrote the *Federalist* essays, Hamilton was shielded by anonymity. He was in this case as artful as a chameleon, and forcefully claimed in *Federalist* No. 33 that, "it will not follow from this doctrine that acts of the large society which are NOT PURSUANT to its constitutional powers, but which are invasions of the residuary authorities of the smaller societies, will become the supreme law of the land." Moreover, he asserted that the Constitution "EXPRESSLY confines this supremacy to laws made PURSUANT TO THE CONSTITUTION..." meaning that any law that exceeded the delegated authority of the general government would be void.[6]

The Poughkeepsie Convention did not offer the luxury of conceal-ment. Hamilton would be face-to-face with the very people he blasted in the *Federalist* and would have to listen to their charges directly. Plus, any comments he made would be checked by the leading figures in oppo-sition to the document in New York. Hamilton would have to be at the top of his game, and he would have to lie, for the Hamilton that had been arguing for ratification of the Constitution sung a different tune than the Hamilton that showed up in Philadelphia just one year earlier.

Hamilton's June 27 speech at Poughkeepsie displayed a firm com-mitment to the necessity of the states in the new Constitution. Hamil-ton insisted that the states were "absolutely necessary to the system. Their existence must form a leading principle in the most perfect con-stitution we could form," and then followed up with, "I insist that it never can be the interest or desire of the national legislature to destroy the *state governments.*" He suggested that the states were "indispens-able" for the Union, and their destruction would be a "fatal wound to the head" which would produce a "political suicide." He concluded by stating that, "I wish the committee to remember, that the Constitution under examination is framed upon truly republican principles; and that, as it is expressly designed to provide for the common protection and the general welfare of the United States, it must be utterly repugnant to this Constitution to subvert the state governments, or oppress the people."[7] This was the last speech of the day, but opponents of the document saw an opportunity to expose Hamilton's dishonesty and took it the following morning.

Governor Clinton opened the June 28 debate by asking for several papers to be read before the convention. They showed, in his opinion, that granting excessive power to a new general government would ruin the states and destroy liberty. Clinton professed that he was in favor of a stronger central government, but he feared that the proposed Constitu-tion went to an extreme and thought that the end result would be the creation of a government repugnant to the security of the people and legislature of New York. It was not clear if this move was intended to bait Hamilton, but he certainly grabbed the hook.

Hamilton immediately rose in protest. He could not see how anyone could be opposed to the Constitution when it was plainly stated that "the word *supreme* imports no more than this—that the Constitution, and laws made in pursuance thereof, cannot be controlled or defeated by any other law.... but the laws of Congress are restricted to a certain sphere, and when they depart from this sphere, they are no longer supreme or binding." The states, Hamilton contended, also had "independent powers, in which their laws are supreme...." In no way could the Constitution be considered as a sign of the apocalypse for the state governments. They were necessary, he said, for the harmony of the Union. But Hamilton sensed that not everyone believed him. In fact, he finished his speech by stating that, "I cannot but take notice of some expressions which have fallen in the course of the debate. It has been said that ingenious men may say ingenious things.... I know not whether these insinuations allude to the characters of any who are present.... Gentlemen ought not...to presume that the advocates of this Constitution are influenced by ambitious views. The suspicion...is unjust; the charge uncharitable."[8]

In a few sentences, Hamilton characterized his defense of the Constitution as a matter of disinterested honor and was challenging anyone to call his bluff. John Lansing did, and Hamilton was exposed, both then and for all of posterity, as an "ingenious" and "ambitious" fraud whose statements on the original intent of the Constitution, while persuasive and consistent with how the document was sold to the states, were not consistent with what he intended to do once the government was in operation nor what he had advanced at the Philadelphia Convention. It nearly led to a duel.

As usual, Lansing's speech was clear and unequivocal in its advocacy for the maintenance of the traditional union of states. But it was the three blows delivered to Hamilton's reputation that everyone noticed. He began by reducing Hamilton's closing remarks to mere sophomoric complaints. Lansing sarcastically classified many of the arguments for the Constitution as "ingenious," and said they were "little more than repetitious" while "others are not very applicable or interesting." Strike one. He then proceeded to attack Hamilton directly. Lansing chafed at Hamilton's characterization of the opposition as delusional. "An honorable gentle-men has remarked, that the idea of danger to the state governments can only originate in a distempered fancy.... I shall only observe, that, how-ever fanciful these apprehensions may appear to him, they have made serious impressions upon some of the greatest and best men. Our fears arise from the experience of all ages, and our knowledge of the disposi-tions of mankind." Lansing, then, differentiated men of traditional power and influence like him from self-made opportunists bent on innovation. Strike two.

These were surgical attacks, but Lansing's closing statement was the *coup de grace*. Lansing credited Hamilton with providing "several forcible reasons why they [the states] ought to be preserved," but then questioned how serious he was in that assertion. Lansing insisted that the "received opinion" at the Philadelphia Convention was that the states and the general government would be "hostile" and that Ham-ilton himself had agreed by arguing "with much decision and great plausibility that the state governments ought to be subverted, at least so far as to leave them only corporate rights; and that, even in that situation, they would endanger the existence of the general govern-ment."[9] Strike three.

Hamilton had to respond, and he did so quickly. Not only did he bite the hook, he swallowed the bait. Lansing knew what he was doing. Hamilton was the most impassioned and persuasive of the proponents of the Constitution. Exposing him as a liar would advance the opposition and at the very minimum lead to a conditional ratification.

The official record of the debates by Francis Childs remarks that:

> Alexander Hamilton here interrupted Mr. Lansing, and con-tradicted, in the most positive terms, the charge of inconsis-tency included in the preceding observances. This produced a warm personal altercation between those gentlemen, which engrossed the remainder of the day. As the dispute was of a delicate nature, and as a statement of the circumstances, how-ever cautiously formed, may wear a complexion not perfectly

satisfactory to the parties; the Editor presumes, that the public
will excuse an entire omission of the subject.

Childs's reasoning for doing this is unclear. He was accused by the
opposition of misrepresenting their positions and skewing the debates in
favor of the proponents of the Constitution. Perhaps he knew that Lansing's attack on Hamilton would destroy Hamilton's integrity and expose
the entire federalist position as a fraud, but this is mere conjecture. He
could have been trying to avoid escalation of the personal conflict to
avoid a duel, but his summary of the event was not published until the
end of 1788, six months after the convention wrapped up business. At
the very least, his omission made it difficult for anyone to know exactly
what was said between the two men.

Fragments of the debate do exist. John McKesson, secretary of the
Poughkeepsie Convention, wrote several shorthand comments about the
altercation. According to his record, Lansing went so far as to show that
Hamilton had favored a federal negative over state law at the Philadelphia
Convention. Hamilton knew Lansing was correct, so he attempted to
turn the debate into a personal conflict. He was "much agitated," and
whined that it was "highly improper and uncandid for a Gent. to mention
in this Committee Argumts. by me used in that Convention." Lansing
rejoined that he "was compelled to it" because the proceedings of the
Philadelphia Convention were "no longer Secrete" and as one of the
delegates to that body, Lansing believed he had a duty to discuss arguments made there. This further enraged Hamilton who demanded that
Lansing "retract" his accusation because, "It is improper to be here
introduced—because if my Sentiments were improper—the Convention
tho't differently." Lansing then called on Robert Yates, the third member
of the New York delegation to Philadelphia in 1787, to verify his position.
By this point, both parties were "in a Ferment" so Yates called for an
adjournment.

Two days did nothing to cool the tempers of either party, as the
argument resumed when the convention reconvened on June 30. Lansing
again called on Yates for verification. Yates finally produced his notes

and read what he scribbled about Hamilton's speech. He tried to defuse the situation as much as possible by suggesting that there could be errors in his summary of events, but he concluded that Lansing was correct in his assertion that Hamilton favored the reduction of the states and that state governments would only be invested with "corporate" powers. Hamilton then took the offensive. He asked if Yates understood the term "corporate" to mean reducing the states to the same status as a city, like New York City. Yates responded that he believed Hamilton used the term as a way of describing the relationship between the state and general government, meaning that the states could not "retard" the operation of the general government to any degree, but he did not think Hamilton thought each state would become an impotent creation of the central authority devoid of any sovereign powers. Hamilton followed up by asserting that he had insisted during the Philadelphia Convention that the "state governments ought to be supported, and that they would be useful and necessary...." Yates concurred that he heard Hamilton take that position. John Jay then offered a cross examination where he pressed Yates on the issue at hand, namely how Hamilton viewed the state governments. Yates stuck to his story, even reciting virtually word for word the same statement he had made to Hamilton about "corporations."

Hamilton now had the advantage. Lansing's star witness seemed to corroborate Hamilton's narrative of events. Lansing tried to interject and offer further explanation but the convention called him to order. Lansing then suggested that Yates's notes be read in their entirety. The rule of the convention, however, mandated that such a suggestion be carried by a formal motion. When Lansing refused, the convention adjourned.[10] This ended the debate, and from the scattered information it appears that Hamilton had the better end.

Not so fast.

One observer remarked that "every person I have conversed with is clearly convinced that Lansing is fully justified...."[11] He was entirely correct. If Yates's notes had been read, they would have validated Lansing's position, and although it seems that Hamilton won the debate (albeit from information gathered by proponents of the document)

Lansing had laid bare Hamilton's duplicity. Both the Madison and Yates notes contain similar language, namely Hamilton's insistence that the states be reduced to corporations. Yates, in fact, wrote that Hamilton said the delegates to the Philadelphia Convention should "annihilate the state distinctions and state operations..." though he suggested that "the state governments reduced to corporations, and with very limited powers, might be necessary..." to offset the cost of sending representatives to a national government and to "carry government to the extremities."[12]

Which Hamilton is to be believed, the Hamilton that publicly claimed the states were essential to the fabric of the Union and held substantial powers to check the general government, or the Hamilton who insisted that the states be "annihilated" and reduced to "corporations"?

Hamilton understood that he had to sell the Constitution as a document that preserved the original federal republic—a union of states—while privately he wished that the delegates to the Philadelphia Convention had done more to create a truly national government. His public pronouncements in both the *Federalist* essays and speeches at the Poughkeepsie Convention should go a long way in helping modern Americans understand his original intent. Hamilton was one of the most vocal proponents of the Constitution in the months leading to ratification and thus his statements on the powers of the general government and the proper role of the states should be widely respected. At the same time, Hamilton's plan for a national government that he advanced on June 18, 1787, shows that he had very little faith in either union proposed by the Virginia or New Jersey plans. To Hamilton, the states represented a roadblock to "energetic" and efficient government and had to be dealt a fatal wound. If we wish to trace the modern problem of unconstitutional centralization to its intellectual godfather, it has to be Hamilton, for once Hamilton assumed a role in the newly crafted executive branch, he would quickly place his stamp on federal power, and his actions would more closely mirror the opinions of Hamilton at Philadelphia in June 1787 than Hamilton at Poughkeepsie in June 1788.

CHAPTER THREE

ASSUMPTION
AND
IMPLIED POWERS

Hamilton's place among the great constitutional theorists in American history had already been solidified by his performance at Philadelphia and Poughkeepsie and immortalized in the *Federalist* essays, but Hamilton was a man of action and theory had no place after the new central government moved from theory to reality. Rumors swirled that Hamilton would be considered for a position in the Washington administration. The question became what post.

Hamilton's talents certainly leaned toward finance, and this was probably the only area Washington considered as appropriate for his former aide-de-camp. He had been one of the chief proponents of a stronger central government primarily because he believed the United States government needed to reorganize its financial house, but there was another highly qualified individual, the well-fed and round Robert Morris of Pennsylvania, a man whose role as the "Financier of the Revolution" made him one of the more powerful men in the founding generation, if not the wealthiest. Morris was a known quantity, even if considered corrupt by some leading men, but he was now a senator from Pennsylvania and it was uncertain whether he would accept the position if offered. Hamilton was a wildcard. He was talented, yes, and a dedicated republican, but he was also young, brash, and ambitious. Washington respected Hamilton, and his support was enough to calm any potential fears.

Yet, as the First Congress got down to business in 1789, it became clear that not everyone was sold on the necessity of handing over substantial authority to the new central government, particularly one with as much potential power of the purse, even if it would create a "more perfect Union." In May 1789, Representative Elias Boudinot of New Jersey introduced a bill providing for the creation of three executive departments: Foreign Affairs (later the State Department), the War Department, and the Treasury Department. Boudinot was a stout, pious, and upright man whose scribblings on religion and morality trumped his political musings. He had served in the Continental Congress and as the president of that body from 1782 to 1783. He later became the director of the United States Mint and was a keen supporter of the Constitution, most importantly because he thought the new document would be a better vehicle for managing the finances of the United States. As a result, he believed the "Secretary of Finance" to be the most important position of the three, and though he thought this man should "make it his duty to superintend the treasury and the finances of the United States, examine the public debts and engagements, inspect the collection and expenditure of the revenue, and to form and digest plans for its improvement," he also argued the department should be restrained "from being concerned in trade or commerce...."[1]

This ultimately became the crux of the debate. After thoroughly debating presidential appointment powers, the House decided to debate each executive department separately so as to give it its proper scrutiny. The treasury was the first to be considered.

Elbridge Gerry of Massachusetts thought Boudinot's parameters left the new office open to corruption. Gerry was one of the lone voices against the Constitution in Philadelphia in 1787 and he refused to sign the document. He was often described as self-serving and he had made a fortune on government contracts during the American War for Independence. His thin frame and high cheek bones highlighted a snide though confident smirk, and his biting wit crumpled even the most formidable opponents in debate. That said, his tactics in the first Congress were schizophrenic. On the one hand, Gerry reversed course and supported an energetic central government, the very thing he opposed in Philadelphia, but on the other he recoiled from the power being considered by the House for the Treasury Department. Gerry favored a Board of Trade over a single individual invested with extensive power of the purse. He also worried that anyone chosen for this position would presumably tarnish his reputation and be subjected to constant inquiry concerning his motives. That alone would scare off any "honest, upright" man, and for that reason he thought it might be politic to search for a foreigner to assume such an office.

The majority of the House sympathized with Gerry, though not with his unique scheme to directly involve foreign interests in American finance. James Madison in particular understood Gerry's fear of corruption and suggested that all powers entrusted to the new Treasury Department be regulated and checked so as to "give indubitable security for the perfect preservation of the public interest, and to prevent that suspicion which men of integrity were ever desirous of avoiding."[2] The House decided to refer the issue to a separate committee and charge it with crafting the powers of the executive departments.

When the committee presented its report in June, critics immediately pounced on the prospect of a treasury secretary wading into legislative business. Led by John Page of Virginia and Thomas Tudor Tucker of South Carolina, they questioned the logic of giving a member of the executive branch legislative authority. Page was Thomas Jefferson's closest friend while the two attended the College of William and Mary, and he was from one of the leading families in Virginia. His views on the powers of the general government were consistent with those of leading proponents of the Constitution during ratification, namely that the general government had expressly delegated powers and that the executive branch would be constrained by the language of the text. Page took issue with the language calling for the secretary of the treasury "to digest and report plans for the improvement and management of the revenue, and the support of the public credit...." He considered allowing the treasury secretary to "report" to the Congress to be a "dangerous innovation upon the constitutional privilege of this House; it would create an undue influence within these walls, because members might be led, by the deference commonly paid to men of abilities, who give an opinion in a case they have thoroughly studied, to support the minister's plan, even against their own judgment. Nor would the mischief stop here; it would establish a precedent which might be extended, until we admitted all the ministers of the Government on the floor, to explain and support the plans they have digested and reported: thus laying a foundation for an aristocracy or a detestable monarchy."[3]

Tucker was eventually appointed as treasurer of the United States by Thomas Jefferson, and his younger brother St. George Tucker was one of the more prominent legal minds in the United States and the patriarch of perhaps the most formidable strict constructionist political family in American history. Thomas Tudor Tucker shared his brother's views and had opposed the ratification of the Constitution in South Carolina. He thought the language establishing the Treasury Department unconstitutionally enlarged executive power. "If we authorize him to prepare and report plans, it will create an interference of the executive with the legislative power...." To Tucker, the Constitution was clear on the issue. All bills for raising revenue had to originate in the House of Representatives. Thus, he asked, "How can the business originate in this House, if we have it reported to us by the Minister of Finance?"[4] This was the pressing question.

Only two other members of the House seemed to share their views, Gerry and Samuel Livermore of New Hampshire. The rest of the House thought Tucker and Page were too sensitive to impropriety and too strict in interpreting the Constitution. Even Madison was at a loss to understand the opposition. Thomas Fitzsimmons of Pennsylvania offered a compromise amendment. He proposed striking the term "report" and replacing it with "prepare." To his mind, that would remove any "jealousy" and would simply require the secretary to present a plan when Congress requested it. His amendment easily passed.[5]

In hindsight, perhaps Page and Tucker were on to something. Their fear that the secretary of the treasury would become a de facto member of the House and would initiate legislation was ultimately justified, if only because Hamilton believed that the members of the executive departments should behave that way.

Washington conducted business with a top-down approach. All decisions had to be made by him and no one could act alone. This comported with the way the executive branch was sold to the states during ratification. It allowed for energy and accountability. But Hamilton thought each department head could serve as a virtual prime minister, or more accurately in relation to the treasury, as a chancellor of the exchequer. This position had tremendous power in Great Britain. It was Chancellor of the Exchequer Charles Townshend who proposed the series of infamous taxes that caused a stir in the British North American colonies, and it was this type of meddling that men like Page and Tucker feared most. Their opposition was based on experience. If the Congress possessed all power of the purse, then the executive branch should remain as distant from that process as possible. Hamilton would not entirely have his way—the recent vote ensured that the heads of departments would not appear in person before the Congress; however, he would be able to wiggle around the problem by presenting long papers defending his proposed legislative agenda to Congress. As in the *Federalist Papers*, Hamilton's gift of persuasion moved men to adopt an entirely different view of constitutional authority, one that was certainly present but dormant in the early stages of the federal government.

Hamilton was appointed secretary of the treasury on September 11, 1789, and he spent his first three months in office organizing the department. No charge has ever been made that Hamilton used the office for personal gain. He was a disinterested statesman in that regard, something even subordinates in his department could not claim to be. Hamilton was a nationalist without sectional prejudice. The United States, not any particular state or area, was his home, and for this reason he often bristled when regional interests appeared to retard issues of national concern. Every action Hamilton pursued, every piece of legislation he favored, every proposal that contained his signature had this tinge of nationalism. Clearly, to most modern readers, this sounds like a blessing, for Hamilton was able to see the benefits of a strong financial system, a stable currency, and a vibrant economy. There is, however, one glaring problem with his approach: very little of what Hamilton proposed was constitutional, at least not according to the Constitution as ratified. Hamilton himself had argued against his own future actions in both the *Federalist* essays and in his speeches at Poughkeepsie in 1788. To get around this issue, Hamilton adopted positions that *opponents* of the document said would be used when they urged the people of the states to reject the Constitution during ratification. Hamilton invented "implied powers."

Hamilton's plan to stabilize the American economy contained several clear points. His first priority was restoring faith in the public credit, a difficult proposition considering the financial problems the fledgling United States faced both during and immediately after the American War for Independence. To do so, Hamilton would advocate the assumption of state debts, higher taxes, a central banking system, a stable currency, and federal promotion of commerce and industry. Of these five agenda items, only two—a stable currency and higher taxes—were clearly constitutional. Everyone in the founding generation believed the new central government would assume the debt of the old confederation, but the question of state debt was not settled.

Hamilton presented his "First Report on the Public Credit" to Congress on January 14, 1790. He opened the essay with an appeal to moral responsibility and patriotism. France and the Netherlands had to be repaid. In the case of France, most in the founding generation viewed repayment as a moral responsibility, and as Hamilton said, "the price of liberty" in the maintenance of independence during the war. As for the Dutch, the United States may have a need for Dutch loans again, so paying them off would maintain a solid line of credit. No one would have balked at either reason, but Hamilton went a step further and outlined why a sound economy was necessary for the new central government:

> To justify and preserve their confidence; to promote the increasing respectability of the American name; to answer the calls of justice; to restore landed property to its due value; to furnish new resources both to agriculture and commerce; *to cement more closely the union of the states*; to add to their security against foreign attack; to establish public order on the basis of an upright and liberal policy. These are the great and invaluable ends to be secured by a proper and adequate provision, at the present period, for the support of public credit [emphasis added].[6]

This list seems benign, but the italicized section foreshadows Hamilton's real intent. Not satisfied that the Constitution as ratified preserved the union of states as under the Articles of Confederation, Hamilton was using underhanded methods to "nationalize" the general government. A solid union of states was certainly the desired outcome of the Philadelphia Convention. Fear of secession drove many wavering delegates to support the new Constitution, but that was not what motivated Hamilton. His ultimate objective was to subjugate the states to the general government, to render them powerless—mere corporations, as he had suggested in Philadelphia.

Hamilton openly admitted as much when he proposed the assumption of states' debts by the "national" government. This, he argued, was expedient because it would alleviate "jealousy," provide uniform revenue collection, and increase confidence in the American financial system both at home and abroad. He never addressed the constitutional issue involved in this plan, namely whether this power was enumerated in any article of the document. He was aware that assuming the debt of the previous general government was constitutional; he provided the text authorizing such a move in his report. But no such authorization could be found for assuming state debts. Hamilton had to read between the lines and was for the first time advancing an interpretation of the Constitution at odds with the way he argued it would be interpreted in 1788 at Poughkeepsie.[7]

Congress focused most of the early debates on Hamilton's proposal on the debt holders themselves and the mechanics of Hamilton's design. Little was said about the state issue until over a month later, but James Jackson of Georgia alluded to the problem in a February 9 speech. Jackson was a hard-nosed soldier, a hero of the American War for Independence, and a clear-eyed sentinel in opposition to any threat of monarchy. He is one of the most unheralded of all the founding generation, due in large part to his opposition to most of what fashionable historians consider the great accomplishments of the new federal government, namely Hamiltonianism.[8]

Jackson saw the risks in Hamilton's scheme long before anyone else was on to them. "The report of the secretary of the treasury," he said, "proposes that we should not only fund the debts that are ascertained, but the unliquidated and unsettled debts due from the continent; nor does the plan stop here, it proposes that we should assume the payment of the state debts, debts, to us, totally unknown. Many of the states, sir, have not yet ascertained what they owe, and if we do not know the amount of what we are, or are to be, indebted, shall we establish funds? Shall we put our hands into the pockets of our constituents, and appropriate monies for uses we are undetermined of? But more especially shall we do this when, in doing it, it is indisputably certain that the encumbrance will more than exceed all the benefits and conveniences?" Jackson described the ethical problem while alluding to the constitutional issue of state assumption. He had earlier questioned the wisdom of debating the issue without first consulting the states and hinted that if the states had been aware of such a plan, they would have rejected the Constitution in 1788.[9]

Debate on the funding plan dragged on for several days as the Congress attempted to hash out the best means of repaying creditors. To many, the issue ended there. Once the Congress reached an agreement on the mode of repayment, the lingering issue of state assumption remained undecided. This became one of the major issues of 1790.

Madison, stinging from defeat in regard to his plans for funding the debt, became obstinate in reaction to Hamilton's proposed "assumption scheme." He and other members of the Southern states, save South Carolina, correctly understood that allowing the general government to assume the debts of the states would be in effect a double tax. Virginia had already retired most of its war debt, as had Maryland, North Carolina, and Georgia. The situation was different in the North. One of the primary causes of the infamous Shay's Rebellion of 1787 was high taxes levied to service the wartime debt of Massachusetts. If the general government were allowed to assume the debts of the states, Massachusetts and Connecticut would reap the benefits of having other states pay off their large financial burdens. This was a win/win for the nationalists of the North. Not only would they come out fiscally sound, they secured a "national" army to put down any type of insurrection against state authority.

Four members of the House simply thought the state debts should be repudiated. This would solve the potential pitfalls of assumption and avoid any type of personal wrangling over who would get paid and when. The Congress had done it before. In 1780, the face value of American paper currency was reduced nearly 98 percent, from $200 million to $5 million, all with the blessing of Benjamin Franklin and John Adams. Repudiation would also give the state governments a fresh start and keep scheming speculators at bay. In many ways, these men were waging a personal war against corruption. It was noble, but doomed to fail as many wallets could be fattened by Hamilton's plan. Interest won out over ideology.

For all of the wrangling and intrigue surrounding the assumption plan—even many opponents eventually enhanced their financial portfolios with sweetheart deals for sympathetic votes—there were some real nuggets of constitutional wisdom during the debates. Andrew Moore of Virginia invoked the Virginia Ratifying Convention. "We are about to attempt [assumption] when no...necessity exists. If that Convention had supposed that it would have been attempted at so early a day, I think they would have hesitated to adopt the Constitution."[10] Alexander White of Virginia wondered why the states would support assumption, for it would potentially "lessen the influence of the States" because they "would be reduced to a lower degree than they should be, while, at the same time, the General Government would be elevated on their ruin." White called this "unjust and unpolitic" and insisted that "the freedom and happiness of America depended as essentially on the State Government as the General Government, perhaps more so." More importantly to White, assumption was "an interference between a State and its citizens, and attaching them to the General Government without the consent of the State."[11]

He nailed the real intent of assumption. Hamilton knew that any plan for assuming the debts of the old government, be it from the general government or the states themselves, would create a system of patronage. He further wanted to employ out-of-work Continental soldiers and put them on the federal dole. Money was the great carrot used to entice support of federal power. Ideology did not put food on the table, buy land, or pad the bottom line. Several opponents of the Constitution during ratification eventually dropped their deep distrust of the new financial powers of New York when they could pocket thousands of dollars of stronger currency. For some, it would also generate loyalty to the new administration and Constitution.

Fisher Ames of Massachusetts openly admitted as much. Ames is one of the more interesting members of the First Congress. He was only thirty when the first Congress met in 1789 but contemporaries regarded his oratory skills as first rate. He was persuasive, clear, and logical, a real testament to the classical education his widowed mother struggled to provide him during his formative years. Ames was an early proponent of ratification of the Constitution in Massachusetts and served in the Massachusetts Ratifying Convention. He supported proposals for a bill of rights, though during his time in Congress he generally favored the nationalist policies of the Federalist Party, meaning consolidation of the states and centralization of power in the general government. But Ames feared the Jeffersonians. He saw them as nothing more than the American incarnation of the French Jacobins of the French Revolution, and when Thomas Jefferson assumed the presidency in 1801, Ames became a sectionalist and eventually favored the secession of New England and the creation of a Northern confederacy.

This makes his statements in favor of assumption and his support for greater federal power more surprising. Ames supported it as long as his people held the reins of government. He did not understand why opponents of assumption feared consolidation. While he did not think that would be the outcome, Ames wondered aloud if war or finance could be conducted without some type of centralization of power. And he used constitutional arguments to defend it. The states, he said, would become *more* powerful should the general government assume the state debts. He reasoned that the taxes required to service this debt would be levied by the general government, thus rendering the state governments less "obnoxious." He also countered that if assumption would render con-solidation inevitable, then rejecting it would lead necessarily to disunion. He could not accept either premise. Ames, however, never directly addressed the constitutional question at hand, namely whether the lan-guage of the Constitution granted the general government the power to assume state debt, though he inferred that it did. It would be several weeks before Ames was answered in kind by James Madison.

Elbridge Gerry did make a constitutional case for assumption. As a member of the Philadelphia Convention, Gerry was aware of the debate that took place over this very issue. Yet, these debates had not yet been published—Madison's notes of the convention would not be published until after his death—and only around a dozen of the mem-bers of the First Congress had been present in Philadelphia. He insisted that assumption of the state debts was part of the plan from the begin-ning. "If I recollect rightly," he said, "it was also contended, in Conven-tion, that the proposition [of assumption] would be useless, as Congress were authorized, under other parts of the Constitution, to make full provision on this head." Even if the Constitution did not expressly grant the power of assumption to the general government, it could be inferred from the document that the assumption power was constitutional. "From this circumstance, gentlemen will see that the assumption of the

State debts was in contemplation from the very commencement of the new Government."[12]

As the issue moved into the early spring, attempts were made to modify the assumption plan. Several proposals were put forward adjusting the amount each state would receive and determining if the Congress would differentiate between states and individuals. This produced several days of debate, and on March 30, 1790, Gerry proposed that all assumption proposals be considered by the entire House. The Congress then slogged through days of heated debates. Hugh Williamson of North Carolina opposed assumption because "the new Government could not be strengthened by hasty measures, much less by any departure from justice." Williamson represented North Carolina at the Philadelphia Convention in 1787 and had been in favor of the ratification of the Constitution, but his measured support for the document always relied upon a federalist interpretation of the Union, meaning that the powers of the general government were limited to those codified in the document. He could not find any language supporting assumption of the state debts and he feared this would be a dangerous and unconstitutional innovation of the general government.[13] Page of Virginia put it better. The whole plan, he said, would "tend to [consolidation], and from that to Monarchy."[14]

Madison then gave the best speech of the debate, one in which he answered Gerry and Ames, and delivered a fatal blow to the implied powers necessary for assumption. "It has been asserted that it would be politic to assume the State debts, because it would add strength to the National Government…but I wish these defects to be remedied by additional constitutional powers, if they should be found necessary. This is the only proper, effectual, and permanent remedy." In one stroke Madison reduced both Gerry's and Ames's arguments to dangerous and unconstitutional innovations. Madison reasoned that only by amending the Constitution could assumption be carried out legally. As for Gerry's assertion that the Philadelphia Convention believed that assumption would take place, Madison questioned, "If, as we have been told, the assumption originated in the Convention, why were not the words inserted that would have incorporated and made the State debts part of the debts of the United States?" The answer was simple. "Sir, if there was a majority who disapproved of the measure, certainly no argument can be drawn from this source; if there was a majority who approved of it, but thought it inexpedient to make it a part of the Constitution, they must have been restrained by a fear that it might produce dissensions and render the success of their plan doubtful." Madison also offered a little gem of insight into the Philadelphia Convention. Gerry may have been for assumption in 1790, but he was one of the delegates who killed the idea in Philadelphia.[15]

So who was telling the truth? This is the key to the entire assumption debate. If Gerry was correct, then assumption should have been a lock constitutionally even if the language of the Constitution did not explicitly authorize the move. That would have been "original intent." But if Madison, Page, Moore, and White were correct, then assumption was an ingenious move by Hamilton to skirt the language and intent of the Constitution and create a power out of thin air. This would eventually be the key to his financial schemes and ultimately the key to every unconstitutional proposal by the general government from time immemorial to the present.

Rufus King proposed assumption as a delegate from Massachusetts in the Philadelphia Convention on July 14, 1787. Like Ames, King thought that assumption would secure the state governments and free them from potential abuse by the national power. In fact, Ames had virtually echoed what King argued in Philadelphia while supporting assumption in the First Congress. There was only one problem. The power of assuming state debt never made it past committee.

In August, the Philadelphia Convention agreed to form a "Grand Committee" to work out the thorny issue of assumption. John Rutledge of South Carolina motioned to form the group in order to "consider the necessity and expediency of the U-States assuming all the State debts." His purpose was clear. "It was politic, as by disburdening the people of the State debts it would conciliate them to the plan." Rutledge, like Hamilton and Ames in 1790, thought assumption would buy support for the new Constitution and the general government. On August 21, the committee produced a report which would have given the general government the power "to discharge the debts of the United States, as the debts incurred by the several States during the late war, for the common defense and general welfare."

But by the next day, the clause authorizing the new general government to assume the debts of the states was dropped. No explanation was given at the time, but when the Philadelphia Convention took up the issue in general debate, Madison mentioned that he thought giving the United States government the authority to assume the debts of the old general government was "necessary...in order to prevent misconstruction" while Gerry urged an "explicit provision" on the subject. The fact that the proposal for assuming state debts was cut from the final proposal speaks volumes in this regard. Madison and Gerry understood that anything not explicitly spelled out in the Constitution would then be unconstitutional. By removing the clause to discharge "the debts incurred by the several States during the late war," the convention recognized that this could not be legally accomplished under the Constitution.[16]

And Hamilton later admitted as much. In a 1792 letter to Edward Carrington, Hamilton wrote that during these two hot August 1787 days, Hamilton and Madison took a long walk where they discussed assumption. "I well remember," Hamilton wrote, "that we were perfectly agreed in the expediency and propriety of such a measure; *though we were both of opinion that it would be more advisable to make it a measure of administration than an article of the Constitution, from the impolicy of multiplying obstacles to its reception on collateral details* [emphasis added]."[17] If the record indicates anything on the matter, Hamilton was being perfectly truthful in this letter. Madison had indeed considered the assumption of state debts an important function of the general government, even as a member of the First Congress. He had insisted that assumption be considered by the Congress and only came around to blocking the measure when his plans for assumption fell through.

This is partly why Hamilton was shocked when his former ally betrayed him on the issue. Madison may have had personal motivation for rejecting assumption, but his claim of unconstitutionality in his April 1790 speech was obviously correct. Hamilton knew it and so did Madison. Had the assumption of state debts remained part of the clause of the final draft of the Constitution authorizing the general government to pay the debts of the old government, the document might not have made it out of Philadelphia. Hamilton's solution, like his other plans for expanding the powers of the general government, was simply to "administratively" work around it by inventing "implied powers." Such powers proved to be the essential crutch to propping up his unconstitutional plans for the new central government.

The end of the "assumption scheme," as it came to be called, is well known. The constitutional questions were eventually ignored after a deal was put in place that satisfied most of the parties in the conflict. Left out of the deal were the "strict constructionists" like Page and Tucker, who correctly warned that assumption represented a cataclysmic shift in the powers of the general government. Hamilton obtained assumption of the state debts in return for moving the capital from New York to a southern location. Details were negotiated over supper at Jefferson's New York home in June 1790. The meeting had been arranged after Hamilton appealed to Jefferson—recently arrived from Paris as the secretary of state—for support in the matter. Jefferson remarked that Hamilton looked haggard and unkempt; and Hamilton had expressed fear to Jefferson about the future of his financial plans. Both Jefferson and Madison saw this as an opportunity to gain concessions from Hamilton both in regard to the capital and in relation to Virginia's debt. In the end, it was a win for Virginia and a loss for the Constitution. Virginia picked the location for the new federal capital and *made* money on assumption. But not even the great "strict constructionist" Jefferson understood the precedent he was helping to establish in 1790. If assumption became constitutional because of a compromise, then anything was on the table. Jefferson would find that out the hard way less than one year later.

CHAPTER FOUR

THE
BANK

The most ambitious, contentious, and unconstitutional component of Hamilton's financial plans centered on a potential Bank of the United States. A central banking system had been the dream of several leading financial minds in America, mostly from Pennsylvania. During the American War for Independence, both Hamilton and Robert Morris favored the establishment of a central banking system to better facilitate financing the war effort. Robert Morris was at one time the wealthiest man in America. He was called the "Financier of the Revolution" and was a leading player in Pennsylvania politics, both during and after the war. Morris considered a central bank to be essential to winning the war, as the bank would loan the central government money, collect revenue, and use that revenue to pay the ballooning American debt.

In 1781, the Congress chartered a Bank of North America with Morris's plans serving as the blueprint. Pennsylvania followed up in 1782 by chartering the same bank within its borders. This was an essential development. The bank could not operate without state approval. While Morris presented the plan, Hamilton's fingerprints were all over the idea. Hamilton had broached the idea of a central bank as early as 1779 and had pressed Morris to pursue a legislative plan in several private letters before the Bank of North America was finally chartered in 1781.

Hamilton's correspondence on the issue was detailed but per his usual style, evasive on the legal authority to create such a corporation. To Hamilton, legality and necessity were separate issues and no mechanism should prevent what he believed to be a vital element in the War for Independence. Hamilton thought that merging the moneyed class with the government would create a steady stream of revenue for the fledgling federal republic and stabilize its disastrous finances. This may have all been true, but the Articles of Confederation were silent on the issue of chartering a bank or any other corporation for that matter.

Article II of the Articles of Confederation stated that, "Each state retains its sovereignty, freedom, and independence, and every power, jurisdiction, and right, which is not by this Confederation expressly delegated to the United States, in Congress assembled." Nowhere in the Articles did the states delegate the authority to charter a corporation or create a central banking system, so by default Article II would have prohibited such a move by the Continental Congress and would have reserved that power for the states. This was a thorny issue for nationalists like Hamilton and Morris. But the primary object of the central government in 1781 was winning the war against Great Britain. Hamilton and Morris both believed that this could only be done with better financial management. That constituted the "general welfare," as required by Article III of the Articles of Confederation, and this was how the central bank was sold to the Congress in 1781 and later how it was foisted upon the United States after the Constitution was ratified.

On May 26, 1781, the Continental Congress passed a series of resolutions incorporating the bank. One stated, "That it be recommended to the several states by proper laws for that purpose, to provide that no other bank or bankers shall be established or permitted within the said states respectively during the war." On December 29 of the same year,

Congress passed a resolution recommending "to the Legislature of Each State to pass a Law, ratifying the preceding act of incorporation; and to pass other laws according to the recommendations, contained in the Resolutions of the 26th day of May last, respecting the National Bank." Two points must be emphasized concerning these resolutions. Congress under the Articles of Confederation passed "resolutions," not "laws." These "resolutions" were non-binding on the states, which is why the Congress had to follow up in December with a request for the states to pass "laws" putting the "resolutions" of the Continental Congress into effect. The Bank of North America would be a dead letter without the complicity of the states, and more importantly without Pennsylvania chartering a bank that would serve as the foundation of the American central banking system.[1] They did so in 1782 and placed the bank across the street from the Philadelphia State House, better known today as Independence Hall.

It quickly became clear that not everyone was sold on the necessity of a fusion of banking and government in the United States. The Bank of North America, in fact, faltered in its brief time as the central banking institution for the United States. This was partly due to tremendous opposition to the corporation in Pennsylvania itself. The constitutionalist faction of the Pennsylvania legislature eventually revoked the charter of the Bank of North America after it gained power in 1785 and then decided to fund both the debt of Pennsylvania *and* the debt owed to Pennsylvania citizens by the United States government. To cover the debt, the legislature instituted a series of taxes and began issuing paper currency. This became a contentious issue in Pennsylvania state politics. The constitutionalists claimed the Bank of North America was unconstitutional. When the Republican political faction in Pennsylvania regained control of the legislature in 1786, they re-chartered the Bank of North America and repealed any legislation hostile to the banking interests of the state.[2]

Pennsylvania politics at this point offered a microcosm of the greater political struggles in the United States, with the Bank of North America taking center stage. The constitutionalists represented the rural regions of the state and were hostile to centralization, organized finance, and the moneyed class. The Republican faction was centered in Philadelphia and counted among its supporters the wealthiest members of Pennsylvania society and the leading men of the political class, including Robert Morris. The pressing question at the time was, if the constitutionalists were correct in their assessment of the Bank of North America, did the Continental Congress have the legal authority to charter a bank?

James Wilson answered this question for the Republicans in a 1785 speech, one that utilized arguments similar to those Hamilton would employ in his defense of implied powers around five years later, and arguments Supreme Court Justices John Marshall and Joseph Story would use to defend blatantly unconstitutional acts of Congress in the early 1800s. In fact, a case could be made that Wilson's 1785 speech was the first to codify the nationalist arguments freely used by "loose constructionists" after the ratification of the Constitution in 1788, including Hamilton in his defense of the Bank of the United States and the assumption of state debts. Wilson's simple though convoluted answer: yes.

Wilson is one of the more important members of the founding generation. He was often called James de Caledonia by his opponents because of his Scottish birth and his penchant for condescendingly peering over his wire-rimmed glasses during lengthy speeches. His republican principles were called into question, particularly after his lukewarm support for the Declaration of Independence, and charges of disloyalty were leveled against him by President of Pennsylvania Joseph Reed in 1779, but his close association with Morris (he was Morris's attorney) shielded him from any further attacks on his dedication to the cause.

Wilson aligned himself with the Republicans and never shied away from financial speculation. He was later briefly incarcerated in debtor's prison (as was Robert Morris) and was on the lam in North Carolina trying to avoid paying his substantial debts when he died of a stroke in 1798. His close ties to the moneyed class doubtless led to his ardent support for the Bank of North America. Wilson was also a future Supreme Court justice, an unabashed nationalist who argued for extensive centralization at Philadelphia in 1787, and a very good attorney with a strong legal mind. This makes his constitutional arguments in favor of the Bank of North America all the more important.

Wilson conceded that Article II seemingly restricted the powers of the general government, but he questioned whether a state, even one that retained its sovereignty, could then charter a corporation for the whole Union. To phrase it differently, could the states carry out such an important *national* function, or does the general government, by its mere existence, have sovereignty that cannot be abridged by the constituent parts? Wilson answered his own question with some creative historical revisionism.

Wilson made two points that were nothing more than a distortion of the historical record, but if true would lend credibility to the nationalist position. First, he argued that, "To many purposes, the United States are to be considered as one undivided, independent nation; and as possessed of all the rights, and powers, and properties, by the law of nations incident to such." This was clearly not the case in 1785. The mere fact that some delegates to the Philadelphia Convention in 1787 sought to create a "national government" on the ruins of the federative system of the Articles of Confederation shows that very few members of the founding generation considered the United States government to be "one undivided, independent nation." It was a confederation of states, each recognized as individually independent by the British Crown in the 1783 Treaty of Paris.

That leads to Wilson's second error, namely the claim that, "The act of independence was made before the articles of confederation. This act declares, that 'these United Colonies,' (not enumerating them separately) 'are free and independent states; and that, as free and independent states, they have full power to do all acts and things which independent states may, of right, do.'" This assertion omits Jefferson's comparison to the "State of Great Britain" and the "Free and Independent States" of North America. If Great Britain was a state and Virginia was a state, then surely Jefferson believed the two possessed equal powers. But Wilson went one step further in his historical whitewashing. He insisted that new states could only be created by the central authority, thus making them, "corporations or bodies politick of the most important and dignified kind." That should sound familiar. Hamilton called for reducing the states to corporations at the Philadelphia Convention of 1787 and was taken to task for it by John Lansing at the Poughkeepsie Convention of 1788. But if the states had to be reduced to corporations by a new governing document, what were they in 1785 when Wilson made this speech? The answer should be apparent: sovereign states. Wilson could not get around the historical facts, but he tried.

By classifying the states as corporations, Wilson opened a new line of interpretation in relation to the powers of the general government. Corporations are not sovereign and legally are at the mercy of the parent authority, in this case the general government of the United States. But the states created the general government and expressly delegated certain powers to the central authority. Chartering corporations was not one of those powers, and though Wilson did his best to insist that the Bank of North America was constitutional, he conflated constitutionality with action. "This act of congress has, either expressly, or by implication, received the approbation of every state in the union." Yet, just because the general government chartered the bank that does not mean it was legal, even if proponents of the institution like Wilson insisted it was necessary. Hamilton would dust off a similar argument in his defense of the Bank of the United States in 1791.[3]

The Republicans in control of the Pennsylvania legislature had the authority to select the delegates to the Philadelphia Convention of 1787. All of the men chosen by the legislature favored a central banking system, with its greatest champion in Pennsylvania, Robert Morris, first among them. If these men could somehow arrange for the new general government to have the power to incorporate a bank, the issue would be solved not only in Pennsylvania, but for the Union as well. It became clear, however, that such a power was not going to be codified in the new Constitution.

The Philadelphia Convention considered incorporation powers as early as August 1787. As in the case of the Bank of North America, incorporation powers were the key to the establishment of a central banking system. The proposed power "To grant charters of incorporation in cases where the public good may require them, and the authority of a single State may be incompetent" was sent to the Committee of Detail for further consideration along with a slew of other proposals aimed at enlarging the powers of the general government. The members of the committee represented a cross section of the United States: John Rutledge of South Carolina, Edmund Randolph of Virginia, Nathaniel Gorham of Massachusetts, Oliver Ellsworth of Connecticut, and James Wilson of Pennsylvania. Randolph had presented Madison's Virginia Plan when the Convention convened in May, but since then had recoiled at the decidedly nationalist tone of the delegates. He later refused to sign the Constitution. Rutledge favored the assumption of state debts, both in Philadelphia and later in the First Congress, but he often blocked the more innovative measures of the convention, particularly those that would reduce the powers of the states. Ellsworth enthusiastically supported the Constitution in Connecticut, but later became discouraged when it seemed the South would control the new government, and argued for the secession of the North as early as 1794. He spilled considerable ink defending the document in the lead-up to ratification, and in most cases insisted that the Constitution would be strictly interpreted.

When the committee produced its report several days later, it had apparently struck the power to incorporate, for it did not appear on the revised list, and when the Committee of Style submitted a new draft of the document on September 10, incorporation powers were nowhere to be found. There were private discussions on the issue. James McHenry of Maryland was perplexed as to why the Congress was not being granted the power to erect internal improvements. McHenry was as much a proponent for the establishment of a national government as Wilson, and he often regarded Hamilton as the true leader of the Federalist faction in American politics. His journal of the Philadelphia Convention, though often hastily written and lacking in detail, provides some insight into the debate over expanded national authority.

On September 6, 1787, McHenry wrote that he spoke to Gouverneur Morris and Thomas Fitzsimons of Pennsylvania and Nathaniel Gorham of Massachusetts about the possibility of "inserting a power in the confederation enabling the legislature to erect piers for protection of shipping in winter and to preserve the navigation of harbours...." McHenry reported that Gorham was against it, but both Morris and Fitzsimons supported the measure, though Morris said that he believed such an explicit declaration was unnecessary because "it may be done under the words of the I clause I sect 7 art. Amended—'and provide for the common defense and general welfare.'—If this comprehends such a power, it goes to authorise the legisl. to grant exclusive privileges to trading companies, etc."[4] The last line is essential to an understanding of how Hamilton would eventually defend the incorporation of the Bank of the United States. Morris was outlining the expanded use of implied powers, albeit through the "general welfare clause" and not the "necessary and proper clause." There was one problem with Morris's claim. It was expressly rejected by the Philadelphia Convention just eight days later.

On September 14, Benjamin Franklin recommended adding language to the Constitution that would have granted "a power to provide for cutting canals where deemed necessary." His motion was seconded by Wilson—Pennsylvanians sticking together—and then expanded by James Madison to include the original language from August that would have allowed the Congress "to grant charters of incorporations where the interest of the U.S. might require and the legislative provisions of individual States may be incompetent." After Rufus King of Massachusetts and Roger Sherman of Connecticut suggested both ideas were unnecessary, Wilson chimed in by insisting that such a granted power was "necessary to prevent *a State* from obstructing the *general* welfare." King then defended his position. "The States," he said, "will be prejudiced and divided into parties by it—In Philada. and New York, *It will be referred to the establishment of a Bank*, which has been a subject of contention in those Cities. In other places it will be referred to mercantile monopolies [emphasis added]." Wilson mocked King's rebuttal and suggested that the power to grant monopolies was "already included in the power to regulate trade." Not so fast. George Mason of Virginia, one of the few voices of reason against the headlong rush into expansive federal powers, emphatically replied that "he did not think [monopolies] were by any means already implied by the Constitution as supposed by Mr. Wilson." The Convention voted 8-3 against the Franklin/Madison proposal.[5]

That should have settled the issue, but as the First Congress went to work on Hamilton's proposal for a Bank of the United States and it appeared there would be stumbling blocks to its passage, Hamilton prepared to defend the institution with the same tactics Wilson had used in 1785 and had suggested during the Philadelphia Convention. If you tell a lie enough, eventually it becomes true. That is the heart of the implied powers argument in favor of the expansion of federal power, one that Hamilton made famous in 1791. It also so happens that Wilson provided the best argument *against* implied powers shortly after the Constitution was signed in September 1787.

Hamilton's proposals to Congress for the reorganization of American finances rested on the creation of a central banking system. To men like Hamilton and Morris, the United States had not yet moved beyond the financial calamities of the American War for Independence. The wounds were still raw and to them, American finances were no better off in 1790 than they were in 1781. If the Bank of North America was necessary to American financial solvency under the old Articles, then surely a replacement central banking system would be needed under the Constitution. The thorny little issue of legality did not deter Morris in 1781 and it did not stop Hamilton in 1790. This time, however, the clear historical record against the incorporation of a bank indicated that such an institution would be shot down by the Congress; at least it should have been. Hamilton's deceptive genius was again on full display.

The Bank Bill did not meet much resistance when first presented to Congress, with scattered opposition from Southern members of both the House and the Senate unable to prevent it from sailing through at the end of January 1791. But the House and Senate versions of the bill were different, and per the Constitution, the language of the bill had to be identical for it to be presented to the president for a final signature. This reconciliation process is where things became dicey.

Much of the behind the scenes opposition to the bank was not ideological, though Madison and Jefferson would ultimately move the ball in that direction. The Bank Bill became joined to a more contentious discussion of Hamilton's tax proposals and the prospect of moving the seat of government to a Southern location. The Senate had colluded with Hamilton and inserted language into a tax bill that would have eliminated state lines for collection districts. By default, Hamilton was creating a national collection system by working around the problem of state sovereignty. If he could not reduce the states to corporations by law, he would simply do it in fact. This made the Senate and House versions of the bill radically different.

At the same time, the Pennsylvania legislature was causing anxiety among Southerners in Philadelphia. If the Congress incorporated a bank and planted it firmly in Philadelphia, it would become nearly impossible to move the seat of government to the Potomac River. This was too vexing for Madison, Jefferson, and even George Washington himself to consider, but the Pennsylvania legislature had, in fact, set aside funds to construct several new government buildings in Philadelphia, and none of the Pennsylvania congressional delegation were shy about insisting that the capital should stay in the Keystone State. Madison saw the Bank Bill as an opportunity to crush this brewing rebellion against the compromise over the "assumption scheme." If the Pennsylvania delegation remained intransigent on the capital issue, then Madison would launch an attack against their treasured bank on constitutional grounds. Pennsylvania called his bluff and Madison responded.

The reconciled Bank Bill had already received two readings when Madison began a two-day legal takedown of the institution in February 1791. On February 2, Madison rose and specifically challenged the constitutionality of the Bank Bill. This was not a case of merit or necessity. To Madison, it publicly became a legal issue hitting at the heart of the nature of the general government. He began by asserting that, "a power to grant charters of incorporation had been proposed in the General Convention and rejected." He then articulated what has become known as "original-ism" today:

> After some general remarks on the limitations of all political power, he took notice of the peculiar manner in which the Federal Government is limited. It is not a general grant, out of which particular powers are excepted; it is a grant of particular powers only, leaving the general mass in other hands. *So it had been understood by its friends and its foes, and so it was to be interpreted* [emphasis added].[6]

The Constitution was sold to the states in 1788 as a document that granted or delegated specific powers to the general government. All others were retained by the states or the people of the states, and as proponents of the document continually argued, any act of Congress that exceeded its constitutional authority would be void. The power to incorporate was not a delegated power and thus could not be legally exercised by the general government.

Certainly, the concept of implied powers was debatable and even Madison himself had hinted at the possibility of such powers in *Federalist* No. 44 (though he also argued against such construction in the same document), but Madison was defending the process of ratification and the promises the proponents of the document had made to wavering delegates at all state ratifying conventions, particularly in his home state of Virginia. Madison argued that only one clause of the Constitution could be used to defend the bank, the "necessary and proper clause" found at the conclusion of Article I, Section 8. Even this clause, Madison insisted, did not grant the general government unlimited power.

Opponents of the Constitution in 1788 pounced on the "necessary and proper clause" as a clear indication that the Constitution would subvert the state governments, unilaterally centralize power, and destroy the original union of states. Proponents insisted they had nothing to fear. The best summary rejection of implied powers from the "necessary and proper clause" came from the arguments of George Nicholas in the

Virginia Ratifying Convention. Next to Madison, Nicholas was the most vocal and persuasive proponent of the document in his state. It was not due to his looks. Nicholas had a large, round, bald head and an even larger belly, and one cartoonist portrayed him as a ball of plum pudding with legs during the Ratifying Convention, a depiction that made Madison laugh to the point of tears. But he was also of sound legal mind and is considered the father of the Kentucky Constitution. Nicholas argued that, "The clause which was affectedly called the sweeping clause contained no new grant of power...if it had been added at the end of every one of the enumerated powers, instead of being inserted at the end of all, it would be obvious to any one that it was no augmentation of power.... As it would grant no new power if inserted at the end of each clause, it could not when subjoined to the whole."[7] Even Hamilton himself appeared to support this position. In *Federalist* No. 33, Hamilton sought to alleviate disquiet over the "sweeping clause" by suggesting that the powers of the government would be the same without the words "necessary and proper." He labeled it "only a declaratory truth, which would have resulted by necessary and unavoidable implication from the very act of constituting a Federal Government, and *vesting it with certain specified powers* [emphasis added]."[8] That was the key. The general government, according to Hamilton, Nicholas, and every proponent of the Constitution, had specified powers that could not be enlarged through misconstruction.

Madison's case was airtight. The Philadelphia Convention had rejected a proposal—by Madison himself—to authorize the general government to erect corporations, and the debates surrounding ratification of the Constitution proved that the necessary and proper clause did not expand the powers of the general government through some mysterious and magical creation of implied powers. But as Madison predicted, this did not stop proponents of the bank from defending it by using the "necessary and proper clause." Most importantly, this was the line of attack Hamilton used in his legal brief to George Washington just three weeks later.

Congress was unmoved by Madison's skillful evisceration of the Bank Bill. Several members made speeches refuting Madison's position, with John Vining, the handsome, wealthy, and silver-tongued patriot from Delaware, questioning how Madison could claim to be the only expert on the Philadelphia Convention when over a dozen other members of Congress had been delegates to that august body as well. Certainly they would remember what was said during the convention. And some did, though not as clearly as Madison who had jotted down his notes of the convention. Elbridge Gerry contested Madison's recollection of events by suggesting that the opposition to the motion to allow Congress to erect commercial corporations had nothing to do with a bank. If Madison's notes are to be believed, and they were backed up by other members of the convention at various times, then Gerry's assessment of events did not match that of the consensus. Yet, the bill easily passed over Madison's objections and was sent to Washington for his signature.

Washington, however, had been entirely persuaded by Madison's arguments. He also asked Thomas Jefferson and Attorney General Edmund Randolph to draft opinions on the Bank Bill knowing full well that both men were also against the measure. Washington obtained Randolph's decidedly anti-bank opinion on February 12 and Jefferson's on February 14, a Valentine's Day treat that showed no love for the loose constructionists in Congress. Jefferson, like Madison, stressed that loose construction was a constitutional farce championed by those who sought to illegally enlarge the powers of the general government. Neither the "necessary and proper clause" nor the general welfare clause authorized the Congress to incorporate a bank. Jefferson insisted that it may be convenient for the treasury to do business with a central banking system, but it was not necessary. The two terms were not synonymous. He closed by urging Washington to veto the bill because the veto power was intended precisely for this reason. This was part of a broader discussion of checks and balances, of which the states had a co-equal role with the three branches of the general government:

The negative of the President is the shield provided by the Constitution to protect against the invasions of the legislature: 1. The right of the Executive. 2. Of the Judiciary. 3. Of the States and State legislatures. The present is the case of a right remaining exclusively with the States, and consequently one of those intended by the Constitution to be placed under its protection.

It must be added, however, that unless the President's mind on a view of everything which is urged for and against this bill, is tolerably clear that it is unauthorized by the Constitution; if the pro and the con hang so even as to balance his judgment, a just respect for the wisdom of the legislature would naturally decide the balance in favor of their opinion. It is chiefly for cases where they are clearly misled by error, ambition, or interest, that the Constitution has placed a check in the negative of the President.[9]

Jefferson's opinion was a pithy 2,100 words and far less detailed than Madison's two speeches on the issue in Congress, but Washington was satisfied with Jefferson's response and instructed Madison to draft a veto message. At the same time, he enclosed both Jefferson's and Randolph's opinions on the bank in a note to Hamilton and asked for a reply. Washington trusted Hamilton, perhaps more than he did Madison or Jefferson, and though he thought the legal arguments presented by his three Virginia colleagues were airtight, he was giving Hamilton the chance to defend his bank.

It took Hamilton over ten days to respond. In the meantime, the reconciled Bank Bill had passed the Congress and now Washington had to sign the legislation, veto it, or let it pass into law without his signature. Hamilton knew that a passive acceptance of the bill would be just as troublesome as a veto. Hamilton thought that in order for Washington to change his mind he needed to give him the ammunition to do it. This would forever change the nature of the general government. Hamilton provided his opinion on the bank two days before Washington had to act, and Washington probably did not settle down to reading Hamilton's message until the day before he needed to sign or veto the legislation. Hamilton hoped to overwhelm the president. If Washington received Jefferson's curt response so well, then Hamilton's nearly 13,000-word treatise was bound to make an impact.

Hamilton wasted little time getting to the heart of the issue. Was the bank constitutional? To him, the answer was so obvious that it needed little exposition, but because the three Virginians had picked a fight, Hamilton accepted the challenge and in his mind finished it by declaring emphatically—though loquaciously—yes.

He took apart Jefferson's understanding of the Constitution. Hamilton said it was "a republican maxim, that all government is a delegation of power." He then chided Jefferson by explaining that this maxim suggested implied powers. Just because powers were delegated did not mean that they were strictly limited to the enumerated text, particularly if the proper end of government had to be implied through legislation. This is a theme he would return to throughout his biting legal brief. Hamilton had been ruffled, and his obvious dislike for the "Sage of Monticello" shone through.

Hamilton then attacked Jefferson's narrow definition of "necessary." Hamilton defined "necessary" to mean laws that were "*needful, requisite, incidental, useful, or conducive to.*" He then rattled off several cases in the First Congress itself where legislation was passed that apparently flew in the face of Jefferson's strict interpretation of the clause, namely in several bills slated to erect maritime navigation aids like lighthouses, buoys, and piers. Hamilton did not have to say it, but even the settlement on the assumption scheme proved his point about implied powers. To Hamilton, Jefferson was being selective in his support for strict construction and he let him have it.

Hamilton summarized his arguments with the following: "If the end be clearly comprehended within any of the specified powers, and if the measure have an obvious relation to that end, and is not forbidden by any particular provision of the constitution—it may safely be deemed to come within the compass of the national authority." Seeing that this could lead to unlimited government power, Hamilton suggested that two other qualifications be met. "Does the proposed measure abridge a preexisting right of any State, or of any individual?" If the answer was negative, then "there is a strong presumption in favour of its constitutionality." The power of the general government to create corporations was not denied by the Constitution, nor was it expressly delegated to the states, so this power was obviously within the scope of implied powers. Additionally, if a case could be made that such legislation allowed a department of the general government to operate more effectively, then the law was necessary for its operation. Hamilton suggested that if the ends are just and necessary and do not violate any rights of the states or the people, then the law is constitutional.[10]

Hamilton's opinion was as ingenious as it was dishonest. Though Hamilton addressed the issue of constitutionality, he never directly answered Madison's charge that the power to create corporations was explicitly rejected by the Philadelphia Convention, nor did he explain how his own words on the "necessary and proper clause" from the *Federalist* essays did not contradict his arguments to Washington and his support of the strict constructionist position. And he completely distorted the purpose of a written constitution, namely to strictly limit the powers of government to those enumerated in the document. Reading between the lines to create implied powers smacks of the British model of an unwritten constitution, a model that Hamilton believed to be the best in the world but one that was rejected in the United States at both the state and federal level. It didn't matter. Washington bought Hamilton's arguments and signed the Bank Bill into law.

Hamilton's opinion on the bank represented a turning point in American constitutional history. While Wilson had explained implied powers as early as 1785 and the concept had been used to justify the assumption scheme just a few months earlier, no one had made the case for loose construction like Hamilton in 1791. Every attorney, judge, or politician who later believed in expanding the powers of the general government had Hamilton's brief for evidentiary support. That does not make it correct. As early as 1779, Hamilton believed a central banking system was both "necessary" and "proper" for the general government to conduct business. He was not going to let the original intent of the Constitution, intent that he helped codify, get in the way of his financial schemes or his design for centralized power in American government.

CHAPTER FIVE

THE
REBELLION

With the bank and the assumption of state debts fully realized, Hamilton set his sights on securing enough revenue for the general government. This would not be easy. The Constitution authorized the general government, "To lay and collect Taxes, Duties, Imposts and Excises, to pay the Debts and provide for the common Defense and general Welfare of the United States; but all Duties, Imposts and Excises shall be uniform throughout the United States..." Hamilton's financial plan offered both a tariff for raising revenue and an excise tax targeting distilled liquor. The whiskey tax, as it soon was called, would lead to one of the most important events of the Washington administration, the so-called Whiskey Rebellion of 1794. This event was not only a political crisis; the response favored by Hamilton and partly adopted by Washington represented a real shift in constitutional interpretation, one that Hamilton had advanced since 1787.

The bill to establish an excise tax was first presented in Congress in May 1790 as a piggyback to the assumption scheme. If the United States government was to be on the hook for millions of dollars in debt, it had to establish a method of raising revenue to retire that debt, and quickly, if possible. No records of the debate over the bill exist, but it fell by five votes. It was reintroduced without the excise clause on June 14, and again failed, this time by an even larger margin. The House cast one final vote on the original bill on June 21. The twelve-vote majority against the bill reflected other underlying political issues, namely the potential relocation of the federal capital. Members of the Pennsylvania and Southern delegations developed a solid front, ostensibly to force the delegations from the New England states to alter their conduct and support relocation. Hamilton's schemes required a substantial amount of delicacy and manipulation to get them through an increasingly hostile Congress. Still, Hamilton and his congressional allies were confident that the tax would pass in the next session once the dust had settled on assumption and a deal had been struck on the capital. They were right, but it required Hamilton to issue another report and to backtrack on promises he had made in 1787 during the ratification of the Constitution.[1]

Hamilton's second report on the public credit, issued December 13, 1790, called for a series of taxes, among them an excise tax on whiskey, to cover the proposed government shortfall of over $820,000. He estimated the revenue generated by the whiskey tax would be about $270,000. Hamilton anticipated that opposition would be swift and vocal, so he outlined three reasons why the tax was both necessary and just. First, while he sympathized with those who considered excise taxes to be oppressive, he insisted the new whiskey tax would be applied evenly and those accused of violating the law retained the potential of a trial by jury, while liquor dealers themselves would decide where the tax collectors could search when determining tax levies. Second, Hamilton believed that an excise tax was best suited for the current political and economic situation in the United States. He insisted that direct taxes on land and other forms of permanent property should remain untapped for the moment because that stream of revenue would be better suited in a national emergency when the public safety required it. He also cautioned against raising the tariff, because the merchant class should not be continually counted on to support the general government. Third, Hamilton argued the United States needed to diversify its revenue sources. It was too heavily reliant on tariffs, and any interruption in foreign exchange could disrupt the finances of the United States government. Internal taxes would not be subject to such fluctuation and would provide safety and stability for the general government.[2]

Hamilton's reasoning seemed cogent, but he sang a much different tune in 1787 as the primary author of the *Federalist* essays. Hamilton wrote *Federalist* No. 12 in November 1787 at a time when ratification of the Constitution was in doubt, particularly in the powerful states of New York, Virginia, and Massachusetts. Part of the opposition to the document came from those who feared the effect of direct taxation. Some insisted that giving the general government the power to tax would destroy the ability of the states to raise revenue; still others saw swarms of tax collectors permeating the land, the end result being the impoverishment of the working class, the yeoman farmer, and the small merchant. Hamilton contended this would not be the case. The new government would rely almost exclusively on tariffs for "a long time." His honest reason, expressed in *Federalist* No. 12, belied his 1790 analysis of direct taxes:

> In most parts of it, excises must be confined within a narrow compass. The genius of the people will ill brook the inquisitive and peremptory spirit of excise laws. The pockets of the farmers, on the other hand, will reluctantly yield but scanty supplies in the unwelcome shape of impositions on their houses and lands; and personal property is too precarious and invisible a fund to be laid hold of in any other way than by the imperceptible agency of taxes on consumption.

He then summarily concluded that, "We shall not even have the consolations of a full treasury to atone for the oppression of that valuable class of the citizens who are employed in the cultivation of the soil."[3] So, in 1787, Hamilton thought excise taxes would be impossible to collect, insufficient to support the government, and would oppressively fall on the agrarian class, but in 1790, Hamilton reasoned that excise taxes would be beneficial, would be justly administered, and would sufficiently contribute to stabilizing government finances. Like most of Hamilton's public record, what he said in advocating for the Constitution did not mesh with what he said and did as secretary of the treasury. A fair assessment would be that Hamilton lied in 1787 and displayed his true colors in 1790.

The Pennsylvania legislature immediately passed a series of resolutions against the tax and questioned why, in 1790, they were necessary. Was the United States faced with some public emergency that the states did not know existed? It also pointed to the spirit of the American War for Independence by arguing that such oppressive and unconstitutional taxes were part of the reason American patriots fought for separation from the British Empire. When the minority of the Pennsylvania legislature suggested that the legislature was illegally interfering with the general government, the majority responded with a blunt retort recognizing that though the Congress had a constitutional right to levy direct taxes, this was not the time, and "that in a time of profound peace with every foreign nation, when the blessings of liberty were expected to flow through our land, there would be selected from amongst those powers the most odious among them, which we conceived could never be called into operation but in the most pressing emergency, when every other source should have failed and sunk beneath the public demand."[4]

Opponents of the taxes could not muster much in the way of a constitutional argument against them. Hamilton knew it, which is why he could so easily reverse course just three years after disingenuously proposing that such taxes would be little used. Most of the outcry came from the South and from western regions of eastern states like Pennsylvania. North Carolina, Virginia, Maryland, and Georgia all passed resolutions denouncing the taxes. James Jackson of Georgia, the staunch defender of what later became Jeffersonian republicanism, blasted the whiskey tax, calling it immoral and a blatant attack on the agricultural class, a group that, as the backbone of Hamilton's opposition—an opposition he had a hand in creating, Hamilton eventually worked to undermine. Josiah Parker of Virginia, one of Washington's most trusted officers and a gentleman's gentleman from the Tidewater region of the state, more colorfully warned that the law would "let loose a swarm of harpies, who, under the denominations of revenue officers, will range through the country, prying into every man's house and affairs, and like a Macedonian phalanx bear down all before them."[5]

It had become clear to anyone paying attention that though the excise tax bill would pass and Washington would likely sign it, the implementation and collection of the taxes would be no easy task. What transpired challenged the nature of the Union and the powers of the general government to enforce its legislation. What started as a tax rebellion became a constitutional question that Hamilton knew would forever impact the interpretation of the Constitution and more importantly the role of the executive as commander-in-chief of the army.

Western Pennsylvania farmers never wanted to comply with the law and did their best to obstruct collection from the beginning. As early as the summer of 1791, just a few short months after the tax had been signed into law by Washington, opponents of the tax began meeting to organize a convention of the western counties for the express purpose of petitioning for repeal of the excise law. Then things turned nasty. In the fall of 1791, on three occasions, tax protestors assaulted someone. One victim claimed to be a tax collector—he wasn't. A second had been sent in an official capacity to western Pennsylvania to collect the excise tax; and a third was charged with issuing a warrant to the men who had assaulted the actual tax collector. In each case, the assaulted man was tarred and feathered and left in the woods without his horse or his clothes. While this was transpiring, peacefully organized conventions had met in Pittsburg and Redstone and passed several resolutions against the law. The two responses were not tied together, but the Washington administration could not distinguish between those who were favoring a peaceful resolution to the problem and those who wanted blood.

No one attempted to collect the tax for the remainder of 1791 and into the summer of 1792, but when an ambitious tax collector began pushing for enforcement, tax protestors dressed as Indians broke into his office located at a private residence, shot holes in the ceiling and ransacked his property. The man who owned the home was eventually chased down and threatened with tar and feathers if he did not boot the tax collector from his premises. He did, and the tax collector tucked tail, went East, and never returned. These western Pennsylvania farmers viewed this as another Boston Tea Party and portrayed the United States government as the British Empire looking to soak the honest working class through taxes.

At the same time, several leading men from the West—among them future Secretary of the Treasury and United States Senator Albert Gallatin and sitting member of the United States House of Representatives William Findley—were trying to engage in peaceful, extralegal protests against the law. Neither man had been born in the United States. Gallatin immigrated to America from Switzerland in the 1780s, was naturalized in Virginia, and settled in Pennsylvania. His large bald head, big nose, and French accent accompanied both a keen financial and political mind. Gallatin disagreed with Hamilton's excise tax in the 1790s, but as secretary of the treasury during both the Jefferson and Madison administrations, he used Hamilton's financial system to his advantage to help fund the Louisiana Purchase, and he favored re-chartering the Bank of the United States in 1811.

Findley was born in Ireland and settled in Pennsylvania before the American War for Independence. He enlisted in the Pennsylvania militia during the war but saw no action. After the war, he became engaged in politics and was a major voice against ratification of the Constitution during the Pennsylvania Ratifying Convention of 1787. He at one point was forcibly dragged to his seat by proponents of the document so they could have a quorum to vote. His bushy eyebrows, smug smile, and protruding nose coincided with a thick, nasally Irish accent. But these men represented their constituents, many of whom were not born in America and had moved West looking for land and a better way of life free from government intrusion.

While an extralegal protest may seem unusual today, it had been the American tradition. The Albany Congress of 1754, Stamp Act Congress of 1765, Continental Congress of 1774, and even the Annapolis and Philadelphia Conventions were extralegal meetings called to address specific grievances and issue statements of protest. They were also highly effective and peaceful. A 1792 convention of delegates in Pittsburgh pleaded with the general government to repeal the tax. Not doing so, in their estimation, would result in more frequent violent clashes between protestors and tax collectors. They also agreed to ostracize anyone who favored, complied with, or sought to enforce the tax. This was a step short of violence, and William Findley's assessment of the brewing rebellion asserted that no one at any one of these peaceful conventions supported the backwoods ruffians. To the general government and the Pennsylvania eastern elite, these protests, both peaceful and violent, smacked of revolution.[6]

Then the tax protests spread. Kentucky effectively nullified the law. The spirit of resistance to the tax affected every level of government and every public official in the Bluegrass State. Not one dime of Kentucky excise money reached the general government's coffers in the 1790s, and yet the state wasn't dry. Kentuckians continued to guzzle homemade shine by the gallon and transport their brew across the mountains to their eastern neighbors. The western farmers of Virginia refused to pay the tax, and in the western part of North Carolina, some tax collectors were harassed or threatened with violence. The same held true in South Carolina and Georgia.[7] This was even after Hamilton reduced the tax rates in May.

Reports of widespread resistance began reaching Hamilton's desk in the summer of 1792. He was incensed and started pushing for a military response that he thought would compel these tax dodgers to ante up. Washington, though agreeing that the situation was "unpleasant and disagreeable," was not convinced of the necessity of federal military action and instead asked Hamilton to draft a letter to the governor of North Carolina, Alexander Martin.[8] This, he hoped, would provide context and would be a softer—and more constitutional—method of addressing the situation. When Attorney General Edmund Randolph followed up a few days later with a firm letter insisting that the evidence did not support military action, Hamilton cooled his advocacy for military intervention.[9] Hamilton also began shifting his focus away from North Carolina and on to Pennsylvania. Part of this had to do with perspective. Hamilton correctly thought Washington would be less sensitive to political attacks on farmers from the North rather than the South—they weren't "his" people—but he also viewed the problems in Pennsylvania as more acute than those from other states.[10]

In the meantime, a burgeoning personal squabble between Jefferson and Hamilton contributed to Hamilton's growing hostility toward the hard-drinking tax protestors. For months Jefferson had been trying to discredit Hamilton both publicly and privately. The charge: Hamilton was the mastermind behind the establishment of an American monarchy and Washington had been seduced into the plot by the forked tongue of his former aide-de-camp. Hamilton finally became angry enough to calmly, though inconspicuously, refute such charges by claiming it was *Jefferson*, not he, who was the real enemy to American liberty. To Hamilton, the tax protests offered proof that Jefferson was fanning the flames of rebellion, and Jefferson did nothing to quell that belief in his private correspondence. But Hamilton moved beyond attacking Jefferson and unleashed his venom on the people who *supported* Jefferson, namely those farmers who were part of a growing political faction known as the Democratic-Republicans, the same farmers whom Hamilton promised he would not harm while scrawling out the *Federalist* essays just five years earlier.[11]

After Washington snubbed Jefferson during a personal meeting in which Jefferson complained about Hamilton's erratic swing toward monarchism, Hamilton seemed to have the upper hand and again put pressure on Washington to take action against these frontier hoodlums. Hamilton kept chirping in Washington's ear, insisting that the opposition to the excise tax in Pennsylvania bordered on treason and was at the very least dangerous to the stability of the general government. Washington finally bit. Even though Randolph thought Hamilton was being too rash in his determination to show the Pennsylvania farmers the stick, he could not persuade the president that it was better to wait and let passions subside before publicly coming out against these farmers. This was a political gamble and Hamilton knew it. He was being reckless, but it was a calculated move designed to squash Jefferson's supporters in a powerful state.

Plans were set in motion for Washington to issue a proclamation on the fermenting whiskey rebellion. Hamilton sent Washington a draft for a proposed public response to the issue on September 11, 1792. In it, he candidly said he understood the proclamation would be resisted and criticized for, "to any one who is aware of the lengths to which a certain party is prepared to go—it ought to be anticipated as probable," but he urged Washington not to waver. Hamilton argued, "Every day's delay will render the Act less impressive and defeat a part of its object," and insisted that, "The propriety of issuing the proclamation depends of course upon a resolution to act in conformity to it and put in force all the *powers* and *means* with which the Executive is possessed as occasion shall require." He considered Washington to be in full agreement that bold action was necessary at this juncture.[12]

Washington acquired the approval on the language of the proclamation from every member of his cabinet before sending a final draft to Jefferson on September 15 for his signature. He wrote that opposition to the tax in Pennsylvania had become "too open, violent and serious to be longer winked at by Government," and while he knew that the proclamation would be resisted, Washington believed it was his duty "to carry the Laws of the United States into effect."[13] Washington issued the proclamation the same day. He "most earnestly" admonished and exhorted "all persons whom it may concern to refrain and desist from all unlawful combinations and proceedings whatsoever having for object or tending to obstruct the operation of the laws aforesaid, inasmuch as all lawful ways and means will be strictly put in execution for bringing to justice the infractors thereof and securing obedience thereto." He then called on the local officials to round up any of the violent shirkers and bring them to justice.[14]

Two days later, Washington told Hamilton that the real issue in the public eye would not be the tax, but the prospect of federal force in collecting the tax. Washington thought that, "the Constitution and Laws must strictly govern—but the employing of the regular Troops avoided, if it be possible to effect order without their aid; otherwise, there would be a cry at once 'The cat is let out; We now see for what purpose an Army was raised'—Yet, if no other means will effectually answer, and the Constitution and Laws will authorise these, they must be used, in the dernier resort."[15] Washington correctly assumed that if troops were raised to enforce the tax, it had to be sold as a measure of last resort, but Hamilton kept pushing forward, and as the rebellion continued to seethe over the next two years, the prospect of force seemed more likely.

Tensions along the Pennsylvania frontier were enflamed during the summer of 1794. In July, an army of between 500 and 700 Pennsylvania farmers from Allegheny County went on a rampage against proponents of the tax. They first destroyed the stills of neighbors who complied with the law and then surrounded the home of local tax collector Colonel John Neville. Neville had borne the brunt of tax protests before, but this event turned bloody, mainly because he had been inciting the violence the previous two days. Neville and his slaves had opened fired on a few dozen militia members on July 15, killing one and wounding several. The militia retreated but returned two days later with one mission: capture or kill John Neville. Neville and the U.S. marshal for the district, David Lenox, took refuge in Neville's house while a dozen men tried to hold off the hastily organized militia. They shot through Neville's house and burned his property to the ground. Men on both sides were killed in an hour-long exchange of gunfire, though neither Neville nor his family was harmed. Lenox was captured and held hostage until he promised to cease issuing court summons to tax dodgers. Eventually the two men fled the state, with Hamilton suggesting this was to avoid "assassination." Just two weeks later, 6,000 men captured the federal arsenal at Pittsburgh and promised to fight any army the general government decided to send west.[16]

Washington called at least one cabinet meeting in July to discuss the events in Pennsylvania. No minutes of the meetings survive, but there was already open discussion about federalizing the militia and marching West. Washington was warming to the prospect, but no one was more bellicose than Hamilton. He was certain that only force would bring these wayward souls back into the fold. When Washington, the cabinet, and the chief justice of the Supreme Court met with Pennsylvania officials in Philadelphia on August 2, the question turned to the legality of sending in the army to enforce the law. Chief Justice John Jay, "expressed it as his positive opinion, that the judiciary power was equal to the task of quelling and punishing the riots, and that the employment of a military force, at this period, would be as bad as anything that the Rioters had done—*equally unconstitutional and illegal* [emphasis added]."[17]

Jay was no friend to the farmer. He was little more than an aristocratic prig who consistently favored the expansion of federal power, but in this case he sided with the original Constitution over Hamilton's more militaristic nationalist meddling. And he wasn't alone. Very few men in the Pennsylvania government agreed that the situation was out of hand. In fact, most thought that the situation was under control and that reports of massive planned resistance to the general government were exaggerated and being used as a ploy to strengthen Hamilton's growing political faction, soon to be called the Federalists. Hamilton himself later said he wanted Pennsylvania to undergo a "political purification." Pennsylvania Governor Thomas Mifflin opposed any military coercion of his state. Mifflin served his state at the Philadelphia Convention and had been a friend of the Constitution during ratification. He also supported the Washington administration and had a firm grasp of the Constitution. Hamilton, however, saw the issue in black and white and argued that the whiskey rebellion was not confined to the single issue of tax dodging. "Now the crisis was arrived when it must be determined whether the Government can maintain itself, and that the exertion must be made, not only to quell the rioters, but to protect the officers of the Union in executing their offices, and in compelling obedience to the laws."[18]

Washington had to make a decision. Hamilton refused to retreat from his open support for military coercion, while new Secretary of State Edmund Randolph (Jefferson had resigned at the end of 1793) agreed with the assessment of the situation outlined by the Pennsylvania officials. The balancing act also involved the Militia Act of 1792. According to the law, the federal government could call up the militia to put down any uprising where "the laws of the United States shall be opposed or the execution thereof obstructed, in any state, by combinations too powerful to be suppressed by the ordinary course of judicial proceedings, or by the powers vested in the marshals by this act...." The law, however, required the president to have notification by "an associate justice or the district judge" that such conditions existed. Chief Justice Jay had already delivered his opinion that any military action by the general government would be unconstitutional, so Washington needed a willing accomplice in his plan to wield both the carrot and the stick. Enter James Wilson, the staunch nationalist from Pennsylvania now sitting on the bench of the United States Supreme Court.

Wilson had always been opposed by the western region of Pennsylvania. Here was an opportunity to further punish western Pennsylvanians for their intransigence during the ratification of the Constitution and for the cold, calculating (though often true) things said against him throughout his political career. This might serve as a final nail in their political coffin. On August 4, Wilson sent Washington a letter informing him that, "From Evidence, which has been laid before me, I hereby notify to you, that, in the Counties of Washington and Allegheny in Pennsylvania, Laws of the United States are opposed, and the Execution thereof obstructed by Combinations too powerful to be suppressed by the ordinary Course of judicial Proceedings, or by the Powers vested in the Marshal of that District." This was all Washington needed to use force, but he wanted to reassure Mifflin that such force would only be used as a last resort. His August 7, 1794 Proclamation, then, was a carefully crafted compromise between Hamilton's itchy trigger finger and the patience desired by Randolph, Mifflin, and the majority of the political leaders of the state.

Washington brandished the stick by informing the tax protestors that the general government would be required to use force should they continue to use violence as a means of resistance to the excise tax, but he dangled a carrot by giving them until September 1 to comply. This window would allow for tensions to subside and the Pennsylvania authorities to handle the situation directly. The message was sent and received. Washington would act, decisively and forcefully if necessary, but he would abide by the decidedly cooler opinions of everyone but Hamilton until then. Hamilton, however, was not going to let a crisis go to waste, and even Washington had already privately decided that military action would be the only course of action to stop the whiskey rebellion from spreading.

While Washington dispatched three commissioners to the western counties to meet with leaders of the protest, Hamilton sat down to pen four pseudonymous letters for the Philadelphia press designed to throw gas on the fire. Signed "Tully," these letters characterized the protestors as anarchists who sought "treason against society, against liberty, against every thing that ought to be dear to a free, enlightened, and prudent people." Hamilton appealed to peace but spoke out of both sides of his mouth. He knew that attacking the protestors would potentially destroy any hope of reconciliation. The ink on Washington's proclamation had barely dried before Hamilton began planning for a military expedition. That is not the work of a patient man seeking peace. Hamilton said as much in Tully No. 3, printed on August 28, 1794: "How can a government of laws exist where the laws are disrespected and disobeyed? . . . . The instruments by which it must act are either the AUTHORITY of the Laws or FORCE. If the first be destroyed, the last must be substituted. . . ."[19] Hamilton insisted this was not the course of action he wanted, but his actions betrayed a sinister plan to exact revenge on these anti-general-government rebels.

It turns out the people of western Pennsylvania thought the Washington administration was sincere in its public pronouncements of peace. They began negotiating in earnest with the commissioners Washington dispatched, and though those meetings did not bear fruit, the Pennsylvania "anarchists" were at least coming around to a more conciliatory stance with the general government. The "peace commissioners" blew that apart. Once they returned to Philadelphia without an agreement in hand, Washington called a cabinet meeting to decide his next move. Hamilton, as usual, pounced on the chance to send in the army. He had already been preparing for it, and when both Hamilton and Secretary of State Randolph agreed, Hamilton zealously began the process of equipping, outfitting, and organizing the nationalized militia for combat. Washington would lead the army into Pennsylvania, but Hamilton was both the mastermind of the plot and the workhorse behind its implementation.

This is where the constitutional crisis began and where Hamilton forever altered the relationship between the states and the federal government. Hamilton believed that it was perfectly constitutional for the general government to raise an army and march into Pennsylvania to collect the tax. Washington concurred, but were they correct? The question hinged on both the Militia Act of 1792 and the actual wording of the Constitution itself.

The latter issue was never completely resolved. According to Article I, Section 8 of the Constitution, the *Congress* may call "forth the Militia to execute the Laws of the Union, suppress Insurrections, and repel Invasions...." That power is further delineated by Article IV, Section 4, which states, "The United States shall guarantee to every State in this Union a Republican Form of Government, and shall protect each of them against Invasion; *and on Application of the Legislature, or the Executive (when the Legislature cannot be convened) against domestic violence* [emphasis added]." Here was the rub. State officials in Pennsylvania never applied to the general government for protection "against domestic violence." Governor Thomas Mifflin was steadfast against it and the state legislature, judicial leaders, and congressional delegation all believed that the issue was under control. Chief Justice John Jay was also opposed to military action. Therefore, the Washington administration had no legal authority to march 15,000 troops into western Pennsylvania in the fall of 1794. This federal smackdown of state authority amounted to a power play by the general government. It was, as Hamilton conceded, a test of federal power. Had the "rebels" come out on top, the power and prestige of the general government would have been substantially weakened, and that would have been a debilitating blow to a nationalist like Hamilton.

But the Militia Act of 1792 seemed to solve this issue when it transferred the power of raising the militia from the Congress to the president. The question is whether this was constitutional. The Congress could not legally punt a constitutional responsibility from one branch of government to the other. All powers granted in Article I are the sole responsibility of the legislative branch. It clearly states this in Article I, Section 1, where *"All* legislative powers herein granted shall be vested in a Congress of the United States...." All does not mean some, nor does it constitutionally allow the legislature to delegate that authority to the executive or judicial branch. Abraham Baldwin of Georgia attempted to strike this clause from the Militia Act, arguing that the actual language of the Constitution made it illegal, but he was rebuffed and voted down by the rest of the House of Representatives.

Others argued this would establish a dangerous precedent. These views were not confined to one section or state, or even one faction. John Steele of North Carolina, a "pro-administration" member of the House, wondered if it would be "necessary to execute the laws at the point of a bayonet." Elbridge Gerry of Massachusetts thought it vested "a dangerous power in the Supreme Executive." Samuel Livermore of New Hampshire, a loyal defender of the nationalist arm of Congress, opposed the measure as being potentially too broad in application. William Vans Murray of Maryland, one of the more ardent Federalists in Congress, argued that the general government was one of "definition and not trust and discretion." John Page of Virginia again provided the exclamation point: "It is not necessary to make laws," he quipped, "merely because the Constitution authorizes a dangerous power."[20] The Militia Act still passed, but it was not universally regarded as either constitutional or proper.

This debate ultimately didn't matter. Hamilton had been pushing for military action since the earliest phases of the whiskey rebellion, and had persuaded Washington on both the necessity and legality of the matter. Force would be used under the authority of the Militia Act. Washington obtained the supposedly necessary legal permission from a Supreme Court justice, albeit a biased member of the Court, and state leaders were either ignored or disparaged for their overt partisanship. Hamilton's own partisanship is often left aside.

The federal response to the whiskey rebellion was not to a clear-cut case of rebellion by "combinations too powerful to suppress." Support for the rebellion from other state militias was a matter of hearsay, and the fact that dozens of men from other states refused to participate in the federal invasion of Pennsylvania merely confirms that support for military force was tepid at best. When Hamilton and Washington arrived in western Pennsylvania, they found few men to arrest—many had been hidden by relatives—no violence to report, and the only casualties were inflicted by the federalized militia against a couple of drunkards who mouthed off in support of the tax protestors. One hundred and fifty men were arrested, but they were all released or pardoned. The whole episode turned into a farce, but to Hamilton it served its purpose. Democratic-Republican clubs, the political heart of the resistance, were shuttered and denounced as Jacobin organizations beating with the heart of revolutionary France. Hamilton had proven that the federal government was supreme, legally or not, and that no state could resist federal power. The whiskey rebellion became the blueprint for federal action against "rebellious" states, much to the detriment of the United States Constitution and American liberty. If the American public could not resist unconstitutional or dangerous laws through state action, the only choice was submission or armed conflict, the latter of which Hamilton ensured would happen in 1794. That did not bode well for the future.

CHAPTER SIX

THE PROCLAMATION

While Hamilton's constitutional maneuverings concerning domestic issues have received most of the attention of legal scholars, his influence on the expansion of executive power, particularly in relation to foreign policy, often goes unnoticed. It shouldn't. Hamilton was accused of being a monarchist, a charge he denied but gave clear evidence for in 1787 during the Philadelphia Convention. He favored wide-ranging executive power in regard to foreign policy and war making, power that was clearly not delegated to the executive branch by the Constitution. In many ways Hamilton was the architect of the modern imperial presidency, for though he never served as president, Hamilton's influence is still felt today. Every time the president makes a foreign policy decision, proclamation, or rule that has legislative authority without congressional input or approval, the American public and the Congress can thank Alexander Hamilton for providing the intellectual framework for such action. It all began with Hamilton's lone speech before the Philadelphia Convention in June 1787.

The convention had been debating Madison's Virginia Plan for several weeks before Hamilton rose and offered a series of "amendments," which he considered essential for good government. This speech provided the best and most concise expression of Hamilton's overall political philosophy. Among these amendments were Hamilton's recommendations for lifetime terms for both the Senate and executive. The president would be democratically elected through an electoral college, but popular influence would be limited. This was, in Hamilton's mind, the best balance between republican institutions and practical policy. "It seemed to be admitted that no good one [executive] could be established on republican principles," Hamilton argued, and since no good government could exist without a good executive, then the convention should look to the English model as "the only good one on this subject."

Hamilton defended an "elected monarch" as being purely republican. He understood "that an executive, constituted as he proposed, would have in fact but little of the power and independence that might be necessary," and he bristled at the negativity heaped on the term "monarch." Would not the executive in any other plan presented to the convention at that point also be a "monarch" albeit with a limited term? Monarch, Hamilton suggested, was "an indefinite term" that marked "not either the degree or duration of power." Men of his generation feared "elected monarchies" because of historical examples, but Hamilton insisted none of those examples would apply to his plan. An executive indirectly elected by the people with a lifetime appointment would never forget his "fidelity" and would "therefore be a safer depository of power." Hamilton's "governor" would have had an absolute veto and though he would have been checked in foreign policy by the Senate, both in making treaties and waging war, Hamilton's Senate would have been as aristocratic as the "governor."[1]

Hamilton's insistence on military action during the Whiskey Rebellion highlighted his unwavering belief in strong executive authority and federal supremacy. He may have softened his tone during the ratification of the Constitution, but he never changed his mind. To Hamilton, good government had to have energy, activity, and a hint of corruption. The executive branch offered the only opportunity to meet all three criteria. Hamilton capitalized on his chance to mold the executive to his design during his tenure as secretary of the treasury. By 1794, he was the de facto prime minister of the United States, a man who had managed to acquire virtually unchecked control of both the foreign and domestic arms of government. He set the agenda and Washington often complied.

As much as domestic issues plagued the formation of the new American government under the Constitution, it was the broiling troubles with France and Great Britain that set the stage for the transformational political conflicts of the 1790s. The Whiskey Rebellion cannot be viewed in a vacuum. Certainly, hard feelings over what frontier farmers considered unjust and illegal taxation had started the scuffle, but to Hamilton and other members of his faction, these backwoods tax dodgers filled with liquid courage were simply a manifestation of French Jacobins who intended to erect guillotines on American soil to start lopping off heads, maybe even his own. That could not be tolerated. Much of this hostility toward French influence in America began in 1793, one year into the building whiskey rebellion and four years into the French Revolution.

American success in the War for Independence had been buttressed by a perpetual treaty of friendship with the French monarchy. Benjamin Franklin worked out the details and King Louis XVI agreed to support American independence with little guaranteed in return. The French would exact revenge on their ancient foe, but the stress of that war on the French economy contributed to severe financial hardship for the French people and the eventual collapse of the French political order. King Louis XVI lost his head, as did his wife, and the French government turned to political leaders with a zest for blood and order. In reality, the French traded King Louis XVI for King Numbers, the tyranny of democracy. Even ardent American republicans recoiled at the violence that began unfolding in revolutionary France in 1793. But before that began, the French government made overtures to the United States, calling on it to support its dutiful friend in a gruesome slugfest with the British Empire.

The United States had nothing to gain and much to lose in this endeavor. American leaders (save Hamilton) had no love for the British monarchy or Great Britain in general. She was an obnoxious partisan seizing American shipping and impressing American sailors. Yet, the French appeared to be no better. Getting into the middle of this heavy-weight boxing match was a recipe for disaster. The United States could not afford to be bludgeoned by either party in the conflict, but the British, as the longstanding bully of the American colonies and with a juicy merchant fleet loaded down with luxury goods, cash crops, and precious metals, presented an enticing target for would-be American pirates. The French also understood the longstanding tension between the fledgling United States and its old colonial master and hoped to capitalize on it.

Hamilton had complicated matters between the British and the United States in the early stages of the Washington administration. Jefferson had not arrived from France when the new executive branch opened shop in 1789, nor was his appointment as secretary of state official until that October. This made Hamilton, at least in his mind, the ranking cabinet member and the one most equipped to discuss not only financial issues, but also matters of foreign policy. After all, trade was the most important component of a thriving economy and the newly formed treasury department would be responsible for drafting an outline for the American economy. Part of that plan would involve international commerce, and to Hamilton, Great Britain represented the most logical commercial ally in Europe.

Beginning in October 1789, Hamilton started having secret conversations with British agent Major Gordon Beckwith about American foreign policy. The initial meeting was arranged through Hamilton's in-laws, and Hamilton keenly agreed to the off-the-books proceedings. The United States had not established ties to Great Britain, nor was Secretary of State Jefferson in the loop, so both Hamilton and Beckwith had to meet with the highest level of discretion. Beckwith assigned Hamilton the number "seven" as his secret code, and though there appeared to be some evidence that Hamilton relayed part of the discussions to Washington, it later became evident that Hamilton was acting on his own and *against* the wishes of both Washington and Jefferson and official American policy. Hamilton's well-documented duplicity almost brought the United States into war.

The first meeting with Beckwith started innocently enough, at least to any American Anglophile. Hamilton opened the conversation by insisting that, "We have lately Established a Government upon principles, that in my opinion render it safe for any Nation to Enter into Treaties with us, Either Commercial or Political, which has not hitherto been the Case; I have always preferred a Connexion with you, to that of any other Country, *We think in English*, and have a similarity of prejudices, and of predilections...." He then explained why the United States would make an excellent trading partner for Great Britain and why France, though "indulgent to us, in certain points," could not provide the same level of commercial security as the former mother country: "What she can furnish, is by no means so Essential or so suited to us as Your productions, nor do our raw Materials suit her so well as they do you."

Hamilton then dropped a bombshell on the unsuspecting British agent. "We wish to form a Commercial treaty with you to Every Extent, to which you may think it for Your interest to go." This, he said, was the decided opinion, "of the most Enlightened men in this Country, they are those of General Washington, I can Confidently assure You, as well as of a great majority in the Senate." Only James Madison stood in the way, and Hamilton suggested that he was "rather surprised" by Madison's belligerent stance toward Great Britain, "as well as that the only opposition to General Washington was from thence." But Hamilton insisted that, "The truth is, that although this gentleman is a clever man, he is very little Acquainted with the world. That he is Uncorrupted And incorruptible I have not a doubt; he has the same End in view that I have, And so have those gentlemen, who Act with him, but their mode of attaining it is very different."[2] Hamilton was setting the stage. Madison was a good man, but he and Hamilton—and by Hamilton's estimate Washington as well—would follow a different course than the Congress in regard to foreign policy, one in which Britain would be given primacy over America's military ally, France. The stumbling block became Jefferson.

Hamilton orchestrated sending Gouverneur Morris to London as an American emissary to the British government. Jefferson still had not been consulted, and though Hamilton liked Morris and the two agreed on domestic policy, within the year Hamilton would be throwing his old friend under the bus in order to protect his own hide and maintain a stable yet clandestine relationship with Great Britain. It is doubtful Washington ever knew the full story of Hamilton's secret dealings with the British or of his double dealing in 1790.

To Hamilton, Morris was little more than a decoy for his paramount objective, moving the United States into a close commercial arrangement with the British. Washington dispatched Morris to London in 1789 without much hope of successfully alleviating the tension between the two governments. Neither had respected the terms of the Treaty of Paris of 1783 and as a result Morris's diplomatic effort was doomed to fail. At the very least, Washington hoped Morris would serve as a conduit for information.

His role became critical when the Spanish seized several British commercial ships in Canada in 1790 and claimed the entire Pacific Ocean as her own. Spain was in no position to make good on the threat of war. Her military paled in comparison to the might of the British war machine, but it had a trump card: a close alliance with the French. The French Revolution had already started, but Louis XVI was still in control of the government in early 1790. France began mobilizing for war in support of its blood relatives on the Spanish throne, thus throwing the United States government into turmoil. The United States remained a perpetual ally of the French and a war with Great Britain would drag the United States into a conflict it could not afford. Washington and Jefferson both agreed that neutrality would be the best option for the United States at this juncture. Morris in London concurred and transmitted that the British and the Spanish governments might pay for American neutrality. The price would be the free navigation of the Mississippi River.

While Washington and Jefferson worked to develop a plan that secured the Mississippi without the prospect of war, Hamilton was meeting with Beckwith and insisting that war was an option, as was a potential alliance with the British government. This was not the message either Washington or Jefferson wished to convey. Hamilton was working on his own, and even lied about the entire matter in several cabinet meetings while the issue was hot. In fact, Jefferson began directing American policy, as was his job, toward a closer relationship with the French. This annoyed Hamilton and he continued to privately insist that the United States thought Great Britain would be the best ally moving forward. Hamilton's covert operation blew up in his face in the summer of 1790 when Washington informed Congress that no direct commercial relationship with the British could be amicably established at that time. Hamilton, however, remained undeterred and continued to press for a pro-British foreign policy.[3]

The French mistook this period as a sign of American willingness to hitch its diplomatic cart to the French Republic. Jefferson wished to move America in that direction, albeit cautiously, but not everyone was sold on a Franco-American alliance, particularly since the French appeared to be stoking the flames of war with every major European power, not just the British. Interestingly enough, Morris had been transferred from London to Paris after the 1790 disaster and became a solid supporter of King Louis XVI and his wife Marie Antoinette. As the French Revolution spiraled out of control in the early 1790s, Morris became increasingly alarmed by the methods and language of the French revolutionaries, both in and out of government. He refused to negotiate with the "republican" government in France, insisting that his charge was accredited only by the king. The French decided to circumvent Morris and deal directly with the United States government in Philadelphia. This had not gone well in the past. One French minister had been expelled for immorality—a charge that seems laughable considering Morris was a notorious rake in Paris who bedded dozens of French women and even lost a leg after jumping out of a window to avoid an enraged husband. Another foreign minister, Count Jean Baptiste Ternant, mentioned forming a commercial agreement with Jefferson in 1792 only to have the secretary of state refuse the matter because Ternant lacked the ability to conclude a treaty. Jefferson also worried, correctly, that Hamilton was again working behind his back to maneuver the United States into a commercial agreement with Great Britain. Enter "Citizen" Edmond-Charles Genet in 1793.

Genet arrived in the United States at Charleston, South Carolina on April 8, 1793, with instructions to scrap the old diplomatic agreements forged during the reign of Louis XVI and start afresh. The French believed that the United States and France shared a common cause in beating back tyranny with republican institutions, and what better way to show the world the permanency of republican governments than through a mutually beneficial commercial arrangement, or more importantly, a treaty of friendship? They had already prepped the American people with a grand statement of purpose, perhaps written by Genet himself, and Genet was greeted by throngs of adoring Charlestonians when he disembarked from the *Embuscade*. He was wined and dined by leading South Carolina families, treated as a real celebrity, and then began a grand tour of the United States on his way to Philadelphia.

Genet was no rank amateur. He had already spent time in London and St. Petersburg as a diplomat, was polished and intelligent, and was considered a leading member of the Girondist faction of the French government. But he was also intemperate, conceited, and prone to violent outbursts. Genet was a true aristocrat of the Old Regime, partial to the moderate phase of the French Revolution but nevertheless a man with an affinity for the life of South Carolina's plantation gentry. The mutual enjoyment of food, grog, and conversation, however, masked Genet's real order of business, namely outfitting American ships to serve as privateers in the escalating war with Great Britain and to gather support for a French-led overland expedition against Spanish Florida. Amazingly, within ten days, Genet commissioned four privateers with American captains and gained assurances from pro-French Americans, including South Carolina Governor William Moultrie, that he would have support for a military filibuster in the Spanish swamps of Florida. When he left on April 18, Genet believed the American and French cause to be one and the same. Genet was gathering allies for a larger conflict, or so he thought. Washington and Hamilton had other plans.[4]

Hamilton warned Washington of war between Great Britain and France on April 5, three days before Genet set foot in Charleston, stating that, "there seems to be no room for doubt of the existence of war."[5] France had in fact declared war on Great Britain in February, just ten days after Louis XVI was executed but also after Genet was sailing the seas to America. The Washington administration was still sifting through conflicting rumors and diplomatic correspondence, but it needed to formulate a plan to deal with a potential disaster for American foreign policy.

Genet was complicating the situation. With Americans already operating under French letters of marque, the United States could be pulled into a war with Great Britain, a war that would be disastrous to Hamilton's preference for a commercial alliance with the British and that might put American independence in jeopardy. Washington had been sojourning at Mount Vernon in the spring, but he considered the situation grave and returned to Philadelphia. Hamilton had already been working on a plan to undermine Genet and thwart American Francophiles from forging an alliance with the French revolutionary government. It had to be neutrality. At this juncture, all major players in the Washington administration agreed on neutrality, but how to do it sparked a constitutional crisis, one that would define the role of the executive branch and in which Hamilton would take a position that smacked of monarchy.

For three days, the cabinet debated the merits of neutrality and in particular the language to be used in issuing such a statement. There was no hint at this point that a unilateral executive action would be opposed on constitutional grounds. Jefferson tried to soften Hamilton's strong language while insisting that European powers should jockey for American financial support. Hamilton wanted immediate neutrality and an express prohibition on American participation in the war between Britain and France, including a repudiation of the 1778 treaties with the French government. Washington sided with Hamilton on several points but threw Jefferson a bone by agreeing to meet with Genet and by avoiding use of the term "neutrality" in his forthcoming proclamation.

Washington issued his proclamation on April 22, just four days after Genet left Charleston. He stated that the United States was to "pursue a conduct friendly and impartial toward the belligerent Powers..." and that the citizens of the United States ought "carefully to avoid all acts and proceedings whatsoever, which may in any manner tend to contravene such disposition." Washington softened the language of the proclamation by resisting Hamilton's desire to enact harsh measures against those who violated the terms of the statement. But the question became, did Washington have the authority to issue such a proclamation, and though he did not provide for any specific penalties for Americans operating under French letters of marque, did he have the ability to authorize the American judicial system to prosecute anyone who willingly would "violate the law of nations, with respect to the Powers at war, or any of them..."? James Madison said no, and the debate that eventually transpired between Hamilton and Madison expressed the deep divisions between Hamilton's conception of executive powers and those of the Constitution as ratified in 1788.[6]

As Genet was meandering north toward Philadelphia—and hoping for a meeting with Washington at Mount Vernon—the *Embuscade* arrived in Philadelphia loaded down with British prizes, including a former British ship *Grange* in tow captured in the Delaware Bay, all of this *after* Washington had issued his proclamation. Thousands of Philadelphians crowded the wharf and gave a rousing applause as the British colors were furled for the French Tricolor. For the next two weeks, prominent members of Philadelphia society entertained Genet and it seemed, at least to Hamilton and other pro-administration men, that this was a calculated move to undermine Washington's proclamation. The pro-French press gobbled up the jubilant atmosphere and suggested that the proclamation should be ignored at the very least and at the very best repealed. These demonstrations of support for republican France put pressure on the Washington administration, namely Hamilton, to defend neutrality. Jefferson privately informed Genet that he needed to be patient, that only Congress could thwart Hamilton's pro-British policies, and that even if Jefferson rebuked him publicly, that did not mean he had lost his private support. During a cold formal meeting, Jefferson had in fact informed Genet that he could no longer outfit American privateers and that American ports were closed to French prizes of war. Still, Hamilton believed he needed to go on the offensive.

He penned a seventeen-point defense of the move in May 1793 that was published in newspapers across the country. Hamilton blamed the rancor over the proclamation to unwarranted partisanship, particularly on the part of those whose hearts thumped with love for the French people. He could understand this to a point. France had been America's greatest ally in her quest for independence, and that spirit of liberty had led many Americans to support the early stages of the French Revolution. But as the revolution turned bloody, he wondered how these same people could turn a blind eye to "the wanton and lawless shedding of human blood" and the "extravagancies excesses and outrages, which have sullied and which endanger that cause [liberty]...." These forces, Hamilton claimed, were intent on "overturning the Government of the Union." Worse, attacks from Francophile partisans were aimed at staining the reputation of President Washington and of despoiling "him of that precious reward for his services, the confidence and approbation of his fellow Citizens." Hamilton contended that opponents of the proclamation hid their true motives. The aim of preserving the Constitution served as nothing more than an insincere cover for insurrection and disunion. These men wanted the government to fail in order to bring about another revolution in America, one closer to the French model than the successful War for Independence less than twenty years before. Hamilton unequivocally maintained that his opponents were clever liars.[7]

As the situation remained relatively uncertain in June and Genet riled up both the Washington administration and the American public by blatantly disregarding American neutrality, Hamilton followed up with a series of seven essays beginning in late June and concluding in July under the pseudonym "Pacificus" aimed at defending both the neutrality proclamation and expanded executive power. They were published across the United States, and just before his death at the hands of Aaron Burr, Hamilton wrote that he considered this effort to be his best work, including the

Federalist, and urged publisher George F. Hopkins to include them in his approved version of the *Federalist Papers.*

Hamilton published "Pacificus Number 1" on June 29, 1793, and it represented his most comprehensive philosophical position on the Constitution since the document had been ratified. Comparing his statements on executive power in June 1787 with those of "Pacificus Number 1" reveals not much had changed, though Hamilton had chosen a different line of attack during the ratification of the Constitution. Hamilton considered the objection, "That the Proclamation was without authority" to be blatantly false. He insisted that, "A correct and well informed mind will discern at once that it [foreign policy decisions] can belong neit[her] to the Legislative nor Judicial Department and of course must belong to the Executive." Hamilton argued that the Congress was not equipped to act as a conduit between foreign nations and the United States, nor was it constitutionally delegated the power. Likewise, the federal judiciary could adjudicate cases arising under treaties with foreign powers, but it could not develop a foreign policy goal or objective. This power, then, had to be lodged in the executive branch.

He then outlined a legal case for unilateral executive action, one that was heavy on implied powers and light on promises that he and others had made during the ratification debates. Hamilton concluded that the "Executive Power" being vested in a president of the United States of America implied that its powers were "subject only to the *exceptions* and *qu[a]lifications* which are expressed in the instrument." Executive power was unlimited except for those "qualifications" where Congress had a concurrent role, namely "the participation of the Senate in the appointment of Officers and the making of Treaties" and "the right of the Legislature to 'declare war and grant letters of marque and reprisal.'" This was not how the executive branch was sold to the states during ratification, nor how it was presented in the Philadelphia Convention in 1787. Hamilton had turned the Constitution on its head, admittedly for a worthwhile goal of neutrality, but the original Constitution became his sacrificial lamb. Hamilton went so far as to declare that "If the Legislature have a right to make war on the one hand—it is on the other the duty of the Executive to preserve Peace till war is declared..." including "faithfully executing the laws of neutrality, when that is the state of the Nation, to avoid giving a cause of war to foreign Powers."[8]

Hamilton was ingeniously skirting the issue and obfuscating the true import of his message, the reason Jefferson and Madison read his Pacificus essays with shock. No one, not even Jefferson, questioned whether neutrality at this point was the preferable foreign policy position—Jefferson eventually favored expelling Genet for his gross violations of American sovereignty and neutrality during the summer of 1793—but that was not the point. To both Jefferson and Madison, the essays were proof that Hamilton had never abandoned his advocacy for an American king. Moreover, not even British law allowed the king to issue a binding proclamation without legislative authority. Congress had yet to pass any legislation on the matter, meaning there were no laws to execute. Washington was, in essence, crafting legislation by decree. If he could do so in regard to foreign policy, what would stop him from expanding that power to the domestic sphere as well?

After reading the first three offerings from the pen of Pacificus, Jefferson wrote a hurried letter to Madison urging him to "take up your pen, select the most striking heresies, and cut him to pieces in the face of the public. There is nobody else who can and will enter the lists with him."[9] Madison obliged, though it took him nearly a month to produce the first of five essays as "Helvidius."

In "Helvidius Number 1," Madison refuted Hamilton's claim that the power to execute legislation gave the president the authority to issue a unilateral proclamation of neutrality. "To say then that the power of making treaties which are confessedly laws, belongs naturally to the department which is to execute the laws, is to say, that the executive department naturally includes a legislative power. In theory, that is an absurdity—in practice a tyranny." The power to declare war fell under this restriction as well. Madison contended that the Congress should be included in decisions of peace as well as war and that such decisions were to be made concurrently by both the Congress and the president. That represented real advice and consent. Madison succinctly described his position by stating, "that the constitution cannot be supposed to have placed either any power legislative in its nature, entirely among executive powers, or any power executive in its nature, entirely among legislative powers, without charging the constitution, with that kind of intermixture and consolidation of different powers, which would violate a fundamental principle in the organization of free governments." Madison continued that only treaties "formed according to the constitutional mode" are "the supreme law of the land." The Neutrality Proclamation did not fall under that category.

Madison insisted that Pacificus could only have reached his conclusions by studying the British monarchy. "The power of making treaties and the power of declaring war, are *royal prerogatives* in the *British government*, and are accordingly treated as Executive prerogatives by *British commentators*." Then Madison delivered a fatal blow by using Hamilton's own words against him. In *Federalist* No. 75 Hamilton reasoned that the power of making treaties could not be vested in the executive alone and that the Congress had a concurrent role in foreign policy. Treaties, as laws, could not be purely an executive act, so Hamilton praised the Constitution for codifying "for the participation of the whole or a part of the *legislative body* in the office of making them."[10] Madison had the upper hand. Hamilton had reversed course—again—by abandoning his brief flirtation (less than one year) with the Constitution as ratified.

The conflict between Anglophiles and Francophiles in the American government took years to sort out. Hamilton had brief ascendency during the final years of the Washington administration, particularly after Jefferson bowed out of the cabinet, but within twenty years the United States would be at war with Great Britain. Genet asked for asylum in the United States when the French government threatened to execute him upon his return. He lived the remainder of his life in New York as a planter and member of the New York aristocracy. He was twice married into prominent New York families. As for the war over executive power, Hamilton unquestionably won, though not because he was constitutionally accurate. Congress eventually passed a neutrality bill, but Washington's proclamation stood and hence became the standard practice for the executive branch. This was Hamilton's final personal political victory, but his nationalist transformation of America would continue in the Supreme Court.

CHAPTER SEVEN

MARSHALL VS. MARSHALL

The witty United States Senator Sam Ervin of North Carolina once quipped that, "A judicial activist is a judge who interprets the Constitution to mean what it would have said if he, instead of the Founding Fathers, had written it."[1] John Marshall was a member of the founding generation, and he served in the Virginia Ratifying Convention of 1788, but he did not write the Constitution, and for thirty-five years Marshall did his best to interpret the Constitution in a manner contrary to the intentions of those who argued for it and ratified it. This included going back on promises he made in 1788. Like Hamilton in New York, John Marshall sold the people of Virginia a lemon. Marshall exemplifies Ervin's definition of a judicial activist.

Marshall, unlike Hamilton, will likely never be the subject of a popular musical. He has no appealing backstory and was not as brilliant or gifted. Hamilton's clothes were sharply appointed, he was interested in consorting with the best families in America, and was unceasingly ambitious. Marshall was a slob who cared little for his appearance; Jefferson believed him to be lazy and uninspired. As a young man he preferred the coonskin cap to the silk collar. Marshall squandered money, spent too much on gambling and liquor, and freely speculated. He was once called "the paymaster of strong liquors, and the barbecue representative of Richmond."[2] This was due in part to his frontier rearing, but with a solid middle class life, Marshall never had to worry about his status in society. His mother was from two of the finest Virginia families. And unlike Hamilton, Marshall never thought he had to prove himself.

But like Hamilton, Marshall considered the United States, not Virginia, to be his country. He wrote during the American War for Independence that he "was confirmed in the habit of considering America as my country and Congress as my government."[3] Marshall's nationalism directed his judicial opinions, and more importantly, led him to side with Hamilton on virtually every pressing issue in the early federal republic. What Hamilton provided in the intellectual defense of federal supremacy, Marshall codified through the Supreme Court. Marshall was certainly not alone in his vigorous defense of centralization even on the court, but as chief justice he wrote almost every major decision that affected constitutional interpretation during his tenure and was only in the minority once.

Marshall was, for the most part, more honest than Hamilton. His plainspoken and forceful manner worked well with his role as chief justice. Everyone generally knew where Marshall stood. His disdain for democracy and the apparent headlong rush by many Americans to support the French Revolution bothered the steadfast conservative. Much of his suspicion for the rule of the people began in 1786 during Shays' Rebellion in Massachusetts and in his own experience as a member of the Virginia House of Burgesses. In both cases, Marshall worried that persuasive individuals—like Patrick Henry in Virginia—could incite the masses to revolt. To Marshall, Shays' Rebellion represented the worst elements of democracy, and he later called his political opponents "terrorists." He worried about a Jefferson presidency because, "Mr. Jefferson appears to me to be a man who will embody himself with the house of representatives. By weakening the office of President he will increase his

personal power. He will diminish his responsability [sic], sap the fundamental principles of the government and become the leader of that party
which is about to constitute the majority of the legislature." Marshall
considered Jefferson's "political system...to be at variance with [his]
own." [4]

That opposition would be manifested in his several landmark decisions during five presidential administrations. Four of those presidents,
Jefferson, James Madison, James Monroe, and Andrew Jackson,
advanced political agendas that were at variance with Marshall's preferred political philosophy. But this philosophy was not always clear.
When Marshall took his seat in the Virginia Ratifying Convention in
June 1788, he was a professed friend of the Constitution, and his several
speeches in favor of the document showed no hint of the nationalism that
would dominate his decisions on the Supreme Court. Marshall, like
Madison, said he favored a stronger central government, but one that
had limited or delegated powers. He gave his most important speech to
the ratifying convention on Friday, June 20, an address that stated his
support for the new federal judiciary and the powers he thought that
branch of government would possess.

One of the issues that raised concern during the convention was the
ability for the Congress to establish a federal court system. Marshall did
not understand why anyone would object to the creation of inferior
federal courts. The Constitution only mandated the establishment of a
Supreme Court, and left to the Congress the responsibility of rounding
out the judicial branch. Marshall thought this was an excellent provision.
One objection to the federal judiciary was that by establishing only one
court, every person to be tried in federal court would have to be
"dragged" to the United States capital. Marshall agreed that this would
place an undue burden on the accused, but he argued more federal courts
"would remove the inconvenience of being dragged to the centre [sic] of
the United States."

Marshall then addressed the real reasoning behind opposition to the
federal court system. Opponents of the Constitution worried that several
layers of federal courts would render the state courts obsolete and create

a climate of federal judicial supremacy, a supremacy that would subject all state laws to federal approval. Marshall called this preposterous, and posed several questions to his opponents: "Has the government of the United States power to make laws on every subject? . . . . Can they make laws affecting the mode of transferring property, or contracts, or claims, between citizens of the same state? Can they go beyond the delegated powers?" In each instance, Marshall answered definitively, no. In fact, Marshall attempted to reassure wavering members of the convention that the federal courts would be an effective check against unconstitutional federal legislation. If the Congress "were to make a law not warranted by any of the powers enumerated," he reasoned, "it would be considered by the judges as an infringement of the Constitution which they are to guard. They would not consider such a law as coming under their juris-diction. They would declare it void." That sounds like judicial review, and it was. Marshall defended his statement by asking, "To what quar-ter will you look for protection from an infringement on the Constitu-tion, if you will not give the power to the judiciary?" This foreshadowed his position in the *Marbury v. Madison* decision of 1803.

Opponents worried that judicial review would be ineffective in arresting a tyrannical federal government. Marshall thought that posi-tion unfounded. If a "federal sheriff" would "go into a poor man's house and beat him, or abuse his family" the federal court system would declare any law that authorized such abuse to be "void." Anyone facing such an outrageous violation of civil liberty could apply to the "neighborhood" tribunal and find relief, or to the state court; and even if the federal sheriff appealed the decision to a federal court, Marshall assured the convention, the federal judiciary would be as impartial as the state courts. According to Marshall, collusion between federal office holders and the federal court system would never happen because of the independence of federal judges and because the state courts would be the first line of defense against unruly federal officials. His stance on the importance of state courts would change once on the federal bench.

Marshall then downplayed the phrase in Article III, Section 2 that gave the federal courts jurisdiction in cases "between a state and citizens of another state." He sarcastically said that, "I hope that no gentleman will think a state will be called at the bar of the federal court...It is not rational to suppose that the sovereign power should be dragged before a court." This power, Marshall insisted, was inserted into the document to allow states to "recover claims of individuals residing in other states," not to bring the states to heel in federal court. This was an important statement, because in 1793 the Supreme Court (before Marshall was on the bench), in *Chisholm v. Georgia, did* issue a ruling against the state of Georgia when it refused to appear in federal court. This led to the Eleventh Amendment to the Constitution, which prohibited a state, or "sovereign power" as Marshall called it, from being "dragged before a court" without its consent.

Marshall then defended federal jurisdiction in cases "between citizens of different states" by using an example that would, ironically, come up while he was chief justice. He posed a hypothetical situation in which a contract for a land claim was disputed by citizens of different states. In Marshall's opinion, the Constitution would mandate that a decision in the case, though heard in federal court in order "to preserve the peace of the Union only," would be decided according to "the laws of the state where the contract was made," and more importantly by "the laws which governed the contract at its formation...." The same principle of justice would be applied to any dispute between citizens of any state and a foreign state, though Marshall contended that the federal courts could protect the states "if the federal judiciary thought [the suit] unjust."

At every turn, Marshall sounded like a firm proponent of federalism. The states, as "sovereign powers," would be secure in federal court, as would the people of the states because the federal court system would rely on custom and precedent in handing out justice. This was not the tirade of an ardent nationalist bent on expanding the power of the general government at all costs. This was a carefully crafted and nuanced speech given to reassure opponents of the Constitution that the rights of both Virginia and the people of Virginia would be safe in the new federal government.

This even extended to fears that the right of various elements of jury trial would not be protected by the Constitution, most importantly jury selection and preemptory challenge. Marshall believed that an express declaration of such rights was unnecessary. The selection of jurors, including "vicinage," would be secured by "the laws of the United States...or in such manner as will be most safe and convenient for the people." As for preemptory challenge—meaning the right of an attorney to challenge the selection of a jury member—Marshall believed it to be protected by English common law, which served as the basis of American law. "This privilege is found in their laws. If so, why should it be objected to the American Constitution, that it is not inserted in it? If we are secure in Virginia without mentioning it in our Constitution, *why* should not this security be found in the federal court?"[5]

Marshall would not maintain such a respectful view of state power. He became one of the leading Federalists in Virginia and corresponded frequently with Washington about the dangers of state opposition to federal power. Marshall turned down Washington's offer for two federal appointments, attorney general and minister to France, though in 1797 he accepted John Adams's offer of the latter, ostensibly for the hefty salary it provided. It was three times his legal earnings that year and Marshall was virtually broke. Once back in Virginia in 1799, he refused a seat on the Supreme Court and was instead elected to Congress after a bitter campaign where he defended Adams against increasingly partisan attacks. Adams took notice and offered him the job of secretary of state. Marshall accepted but did little in that office. When the opportunity arose for Adams to appoint Marshall as chief justice of the Supreme Court, he jumped at the chance. This was one of the most important political developments of the early federal period, and was as transformational as Hamilton's appointment as secretary of the treasury. No man would do more to strengthen the power of the federal government vis-à-vis the states in the nineteenth century than John Marshall. Hamilton would serve as his intellectual inspiration, and like Hamilton, he would renege on virtually every promise he made to the Virginia Ratifying Convention in 1788.

CHAPTER EIGHT

JUDICIAL REVIEW AND CONTRACTS

The Marshall court marked a watershed in American constitutional history. Hamilton's program of national supremacy had met congressional resistance, but very little of it—if any—had been challenged in court. The majority of the state courts continued to practice what is known as judicial review, and Marshall as well as other leading proponents of the Constitution argued that the federal judiciary would be the logical backstop to arrest unconstitutional legislation. The 1796 decision of *Hylton v. United States* represented the first time the Supreme Court upheld the constitutionality of a federal law. Hamilton was directly involved. Though in ill health, he gave a three-hour defense of his carriage tax in the Supreme Court, a tax that Madison passionately insisted was unconstitutional before the bill passed the Congress. The court sided with Hamilton, and judicial review of federal law was born. But this was not the end of the issue. The Marshall Court, namely Marshall himself, would codify not only judicial review of *federal* legislation, but also of *state* legislation. Both positions met considerable opposition.

Two years after the *Hylton* decision was handed down, Congress passed a series of laws known as the Alien and Sedition Acts. More than anything, these laws prevented free and fair elections. The Sedition Act made it a crime to publish anything bringing the president or Congress into disrepute. The lingering trouble with the French Republic coupled with Federalist paranoia over blood-drenched Jacobin terrorists roaming the American countryside led to an overreaction by both the John Adams administration and the Federalist-controlled Congress. They believed these boogeymen had to be silenced and purged or the United States would collapse. As a result, several Republican newspaper editors were arrested and fined for violating the Sedition Act, including Benjamin Franklin's grandson, Benjamin Bache. His *Philadelphia Aurora* became a stinging gadfly on the rump of Federalist legislators, who he accused of destroying the federal republic. He and other men like him had to be silenced.

Any reasonable person knew the acts violated the First and Tenth Amendments to the Constitution. "Congress shall make no law...abridging the freedom of speech, or of the press..." obviously invalidated the Sedition Law, and the Tenth Amendment's express declaration that all "powers not delegated to the United States by the Constitution, nor prohibited by it to the States, are reserved to the States respectively, or to the people" led many Americans to question whether the general government had the legal authority to pass the Alien and Sedition Acts. The power to regulate the press was not enumerated in Article I, Section 8. The question became how to block this legislation from taking effect. Congress passed the offensive bills and Adams signed them into law. That left only two potential methods of resistance: the federal judiciary or the states themselves.

Jefferson and Madison solved the dilemma by authoring what became known as the Virginia and Kentucky Resolutions. Written in secret and presented in the Virginia and Kentucky legislatures by surrogates, the resolutions clarified the division of power under the original Constitution. The states, Jefferson and Madison insisted, had the authority as members of a constitutional compact to judge the constitutionality of federal legislation themselves, and if they deemed a federal law to be unconstitutional, a nullification of that act *within the state itself* was the "rightful remedy." Both men hoped their solution to a blatantly unconstitutional federal legislation would spread like wildfire to the other states. It didn't. States controlled by Federalists quickly issued rebuttals to the resolutions, while others refused to follow suit.

Marshall, still living in Paris as minister to France, may have helped pen the minority response to the legislation in the Virginia House of Delegates. Presented in 1799 by "Light Horse" Harry Lee (father of Confederate General Robert E. Lee, and perhaps the primary author), the Minority Report maintained that the Constitution had to be interpreted liberally or it would fail to adequately protect both the interests and safety of the states and the general government. Included in these expansive powers was the implied ability of the general government to take "necessary and proper" steps for punishing individuals who intended to harm the country. This had been the rub of the entire Hamiltonian program. Hamilton's artful invention of implied powers was now being stretched to encompass not only taxes and banking legislation, but laws that were designed to crush political dissent.

Neither Jefferson nor Madison had any faith in the federal court system to rectify these outrageous violations of civil liberties and thus viewed the states as the only hedge against unconstitutional federal legislation. The federal court system had only declared one federal law to be constitutional. It had not been used to invalidate any federal legislation. Proponents of the Virginia and Kentucky Resolutions did not think it wise to wait for federal intervention on the matter and, as Jefferson wrote in the Kentucky Resolution, they worried that if the federal government were given exclusive authority to review its own legislation, the result would typically be the illegal expansion of federal power.

Shortly before President Adams left office in 1801, the Congress passed a new Judiciary Act. This law added several new federal judges to the bench and allowed Adams to appoint loyal Federalists to these new positions. Among them was John Marshall, the sitting secretary of state and now the appointee for chief justice of the Supreme Court. He held both positions concurrently for a brief time. This would come back to bite him later. The act also reduced the Supreme Court from six justices to five (thus rendering it impossible, at least in the short term, for Jefferson to appoint anyone to the court), relieved the Supreme Court justices from the burden of "riding the circuit," that is having to preside over circuit courts in addition to their duty on the Supreme Court, and expanded Section 25 of the Judiciary Act of 1789. This broadened the role of federal courts and was done to enhance the supremacy of federal courts in relation to state courts, state judges, and state laws. Now state laws would face more scrutiny from federal judges, and in essence the federal courts were provided with a "negative" of state law, something Marshall himself swore would never happen during the Virginia Ratifying Convention in 1788. The 1801 Judiciary Act was nothing more than a partisan attempt to thwart the political ambitions of the incoming Congress, now controlled by the Republican faction, and newly-elected President Thomas Jefferson.

Almost immediately after taking office, the new members of Congress went to work dismantling the Federalist legislative program with the first item of business being the repeal of the Judiciary Act. During Adams's rush to fill the newly created federal judgeships, he had relied on Secretary of State Marshall to deliver the appointments. Marshall was overwhelmed and left office with a stack of undelivered appointments on his desk waiting for Thomas Jefferson when he assumed office. Marshall did not think much of it and believed the next secretary of state would be required to deliver the appointments and fill the positions. Not so fast. Jefferson argued that undelivered appointments were as good as dead. He refused to send them out. Jefferson obviously took this position because it allowed him to curtail Federalist influence in the federal court system and strike down, without legislation, several of John Adams's "midnight judges."

Four men failed to receive their appointments as justices of the peace in the District of Columbia, among them William Marbury. For ten months they waited for their papers to be delivered and for ten months they failed to show up. Several leading Federalists persuaded them to seek a writ of mandamus (Latin for "we command") with the Supreme Court demanding that Secretary of State James Madison deliver their appointments. Marbury reluctantly agreed and the case of *Marbury v. Madison* was born. By seeking a writ of mandamus, the Federalists behind the case were implicitly insisting that President Jefferson and the secretary of state were inferior to both the Congress and the Supreme Court. Jefferson may have agreed with the former, but knowing the Federalist influence on the federal courts, Jefferson chafed at the idea that he could be politically and publicly rebuked by the judicial branch.

It was a year before the Supreme Court took up the case, but it was the first order of business at the opening of the 1803 session. Though Marshall was the center of the debate, he characteristically showed up late and disheveled. He was the man who failed to deliver Marbury's appointment and thus had both a personal and professional interest in the matter. An honest man without an axe to grind might have recused himself, but Marshall saw this as an opportunity to lecture Jefferson and Madison on the law, or in other words to tell the executive branch "what the law is." That is exactly what Marshall did.

Marshall issued the unanimous majority decision and delivered it himself on February 24, 1803. The key issue in the case was whether the Supreme Court had the authority to issue a writ of mandamus. Marshall began by issuing a series of statements that would define and codify the relationship between the federal judiciary and the other branches of government, including the states. First, Marshall "emphatically" declared that it was "the duty of the Judicial Department to say what the law is. Those who apply the rule to particular cases must, of necessity, expound and interpret the rule. If two laws conflict with each other, the Court must decide on the operation of each." This short statement established federal judicial review, but at this point only regarding *federal* not *state* law. Second, he underscored that, "If, then, the courts are to regard the Constitution, and the Constitution is superior to any ordinary act of the legislature, the Constitution, and not such ordinary act, must govern the case to which they both apply." Marshall concluded that because the Judiciary Act of 1789 conflicted with Article III of the Constitution regarding the ability of Congress to grant the Supreme Court the power to issue a writ of mandamus, that portion of the law was unconstitutional and therefore invalid.

Any modern conservative reading the decision would stand up and applaud Marshall's dogged insistence on adhering to the text of the document when making the decision. After all, Marshall correctly argued that,

> The powers of the legislature are defined, and limited; and that those limits may not be mistaken, or forgotten, the constitution is written. To what purpose are powers limited, and to what purpose is that limitation committed to writing, if these limits may, at any time, be passed by those intended to be restrained? The distinction, between a government with limited and unlimited powers, is abolished, if those limits do not confine the persons on whom they are imposed, and if acts prohibited and acts allowed, are of equal obligation. It is a proposition too plain to be contested, that the constitution controls any legislative act repugnant to it; or, that the legislature may alter the constitution by an ordinary act.

He continued by stating, "Those then who controvert the principle that the constitution is to be considered, in court, as a paramount law, are reduced to the necessity of maintaining that courts must close their eyes on the constitution, and see only the law. This doctrine would subvert the very foundation of all written constitutions...It would be giving the legislature a practical and real omnipotence."[1]

This sounds a lot like strict construction. Marshall was, in fact, praised by Patrick Henry during the Virginia Ratifying Convention for his staunch belief that an independent federal judiciary would strike down blatantly unconstitutional legislation. It had now done so, thus protecting the Constitution from illegal acts of Congress. But what Marshall had ultimately done was undermine the arguments both Jefferson and Madison made in the Virginia and Kentucky Resolutions, and he knew it. If the federal judiciary had *exclusive* power to judge the acts of both the legislative and executive branches as Marshall insisted it had, there was no power under the sun to stop it from (unconstitutionally) becoming the most powerful branch of government and from running roughshod over the states. Jefferson viewed the states as a fourth leg of government with the ability and duty to legislate in all matters not expressly delegated to the general government. He said as much in a letter to Abigail Adams in 1804:

> Nor does the opinion of the unconstitutionality and consequent nullity of that law remove all restraint from the overwhelming torrent of slander which is confounding all vice and virtue, all truth and falsehood in the US. The power to do that is fully possessed by the several state-legislatures. It was reserved to them, and was denied to the general government, by the constitution according to our construction of it. While we deny that Congress have a right to controul [sic] the freedom of the press, we have ever asserted the right of the states, and their exclusive right, to do so. They have accordingly, all of them, made provisions for punishing slander, which those who have time and inclination resort to for the vindication of their characters. In general the state laws appear to have made the presses responsible for slander as far as is consistent with their useful freedom. In those states where they do not admit even the truth of allegations to protect the printer, they have gone too far.[2]

Furthermore, the power of judicial review was an *assumed* power of the court not expressly granted by the text of the document. Judicial review, like Hamilton's system, was an implied power. And because the court had been politicized in the months before Jefferson's inauguration, it was now the home of unelected political hacks insistent on bending the Constitution to meet their political agenda.

A leading Republican newspaper in Boston sniffed this out and cautioned its readers to accept the decision at their own peril. "The efforts of *federalism* to exalt the Judiciary over the Executive and Legislature, and to give that favorite department a political character and influence, may operate for a time to come, as it has already, to the promotion of one party and the depression of the other.... Politics are more improper and dangerous in a Court of justice...than in the pulpit."[3]

Another series of letters written anonymously and published under the pseudonym "An Unlearned Layman" in the *Washington Federalist* spotted the real flaws in Marshall's reasoning. "If it had been intended to confer this pre-eminent power [judicial review] on the judiciary would not those great and wise men, who composed the convention, have given it by *marked* expression, as they have given to the President, the *limited* veto, and not left them to assume, as they now do, from *interference*, the *unlimited*?" The author then attacked Marshall's declaration that the federal court system had the ultimate authority to serve as the legal backstop for all constitutional questions. "Such an interpretation, not only corrupts the text, but destroys the compact. There is enough to satisfy these words without resorting to this broad construction. The clause must refer, solely, to questions *properly judiciary*, and, not to those, which impinge upon legislative jurisdiction...." The writer understood that Congress may pass illegal acts, but he did not believe it was the job of the federal judiciary to arrest such tyranny. "No sir, when it comes to this, other tribunals than five judges must be resorted to. A people who deserve liberty and have it ought to know how to preserve it; if they do not and willingly bend their neck to the yoke, they ought to lose it...."[4]

Judicial review was discussed at the Philadelphia Convention of 1787. Very few delegates supported it and most thought it was not one of the enumerated powers of the federal judiciary. Two lesser-known delegates made convincing arguments against the potential for judicial oversight of federal law. Gunning Bedford of Delaware declared that, "The Representatives of the People were the best judges of what was for their interest, and ought to be under no external controul [sic] whatever." To contemporaries, Bedford's portly frame, youthful appearance, and goodnatured temperament belied his commanding voice and powerful intellect. No one stood more firmly for the equality of the states and the limitation on executive and judicial powers than Bedford. He was joined by John Mercer from Maryland, a man who hailed from an old Virginia family who viewed extensive federal power with suspicion. Like Bedford, Mercer "disapproved of the doctrine, that the judges, as expositors of the Constitution, should have authority to declare a law void. He thought laws ought to be well and cautiously made, and then be uncontrollable."

Two more prominent delegates had the final word. John Dickinson of Delaware, the tall, slender one-time Quaker and prominent defender of "experience" against the damaging potential of "reason," believed "no such power [of judicial review] ought to exist." At the same time, he was not sure what would replace it. Madison rejoined that judicial review offered too much potential for abuse, and thought that the practice should be "limited to cases of a judiciary nature. The right of expounding the Constitution, in cases not of this nature, ought not to be given to that department."[5] But what did Madison mean by "limited to cases of a judiciary nature?" Madison and other members of the founding generation thought that the Supreme Court, as an appellate court, could only invalidate the decisions of lower federal courts in relation to law and fact, meaning it did not have the ability to interpret the constitutionality of the law, only whether the party in question violated the law or was given a fair trial.

This is how Jefferson interpreted judicial review as well. Jefferson wrote in the same letter to Abigail Adams in 1804 that, "Nothing in the Constitution has given [the judges] a right to decide for the Executive, more than to the Executive to decide for them...The opinion which gives to the judges the right to decide what laws are constitutional, and what not, not only for themselves in their own sphere of action, but for the legislature and executive also, in their spheres, would make the judiciary a despotic branch." Twenty years later, Jefferson reiterated that, "The practice of Judge Marshall, of travelling out of his case to prescribe what the law would be in a moot case not before the court, is very irregular and very censurable...this case of Marbury and Madison is continually cited by bench and bar, as if it were settled law, without any animadversion on its being merely an obiter dissertation of the Chief Justice."[6] Roger Sherman of Connecticut, known as "The Atlas" for his stern character and unflinching principles, said it best at the Philadelphia Convention when he "disapproved of judges meddling in politics and parties."[7]

Yet, judicial review was also discussed in the state ratifying conventions, and if that benchmark is used to provide original intent, it was clear that proponents of the Constitution believed the practice would be utilized by the federal court system, at least in regard to *federal* and not *state* law. Marshall said so in Virginia. James Wilson argued before the Pennsylvania Ratifying Convention that, "If a law should be made inconsistent with those powers vested by this instrument in Congress, the judges...will declare such law to be null and void...Any thing, therefore, that shall be enacted by Congress contrary [to the Constitution] will not have the force of law."[8] Oliver Ellsworth reasoned in the Connecticut Ratifying Convention that, "if the general legislature should at any time overleap their limits, the judicial department is a constitutional check...."[9] And William Richardson Davie insisted in the North Carolina Ratifying Convention that the "judicial power should be coextensive with the legislative" in order to "correct and counteract" bad laws.[10] Neither Ellsworth nor Davie were political lightweights. Ellsworth would serve as a United States senator and third chief justice of the United States. Marshall replaced him. Davie was governor of North Carolina and founder of the University of North Carolina. Their opinions carried weight.

So if the entire ratification process is considered, Marshall's decision to invoke judicial review in the Marbury case should have been no surprise to most Americans—they had counted on it—but it did represent a threat to state power and the ability of the states to check unconstitutional acts by the general government. Jefferson and Madison answered Dickinson's query as to where to vest this authority through the Virginia and Kentucky Resolutions. What Marshall did with judicial review next, however, was something the founding generation, both in the Philadelphia Convention and the state ratifying conventions, had outright rejected. This brought Hamilton's vision of reducing the states to mere corporate powers of the central authority to fruition. Marshall's court would invalidate a state law.

In 1795, the Georgia legislature sold nearly 35 million acres of land to four land companies in what was called the Yazoo River country for $500,000. This rich farmland later became the states of Mississippi and Alabama, and the shareholders of these four companies were destined to make millions off future partition of the land. There was one glaring problem. Several of the members of the Georgia state legislature were bribed by the land companies with promises of stock if they would vote to secure the deal. Among those involved in the scandal was Supreme Court Justice James Wilson. In fact, several of the men who ultimately profited from the acquisition called Pennsylvania home.

This was graft at its highest and most corrupt level. When the people of Georgia caught wind of the deal they instantly rallied around anti-Yazoo candidates for state office and voted the perpetrators out. The newly-installed governor, Jared Irwin, signed legislation repealing the Yazoo deal and nullifying the land contracts in 1796. There was one problem. In the year between the original deal and the repeal of the law in 1796, several of the original investors who bought the land at around one penny per acre sold their claims to supposedly innocent second and third parties. The "innocent" investors cried foul. Georgia offered to repay investors, but several refused the cash and preferred to keep the land. Six years later, Georgia ceded its western land to the general government. The dispute between the state and those "innocent" investors who desired to keep their land had not been settled and part of the requirements of the cession stipulated that the federal government come up with a way to satisfy outstanding claims of the "innocent" investors. The Jefferson administration established a commission to recommend a "compromise on reasonable terms," but Congress, led by the eccentric Southern aristocrat John Randolph of Roanoke, blocked a bill which would have awarded the investors nearly 5 million acres of land.

The Yazoo scandal then languished for several years in Congress, as it remained unable to solve the problem. In 1807, the scandal finally landed in federal court after two men had become engaged in a legal dispute surrounding the 1795 deal. John Peck of Massachusetts, one of the original investors, sold Robert Fletcher of New Hampshire 15,000 acres of land for $3,000. This was a financial coup as Peck had only paid $225 for the original tract. When Governor Irwin and the Georgia legislature repealed the Yazoo legislation, Fletcher was without his land and his cash. Peck, however, was still living high on the hog. Fletcher was one of the "innocent" investors who hoped to find relief in Congress. "Innocent" was a relative term. Fletcher and Peck may have been colluding in the hope that the federal court system would validate the original deal and thus provide a hefty profit for both men. The land Fletcher owned was worth more than the $3,000 he originally paid for it.

In 1809 the case wound up in Marshall's court. The entire court seemed convinced that Congress was punting its responsibility and wanted another branch of government to deal with the problem. Marshall decided to postpone the decision until 1810. Superficially, the case of *Fletcher v. Peck* centered on the so-called "contract clause" of the Constitution, but the real issue at hand was whether the federal court system could invalidate a state law. This was something Marshall insisted would never happen in the Virginia Ratifying Convention, and when the Philadelphia Convention discussed the potential of a federal negative of state law, the proceedings nearly ground to a standstill. John Rutledge of South Carolina stated during the heated debate on the topic, "If nothing else, this alone would damn, and ought to damn, the Constitution. Will any state ever agree to be bound hand and foot in this manner? It is worse than making mere corporations of them, whose by-laws would not be subject to this shackle."[11] Not surprisingly, only James Wilson was for it, though Hamilton probably would have supported the idea as well had he still been present at the convention.

Marshall may have wanted to avoid the decision due to the potential for an angry political fallout, but he eagerly used the opportunity to broaden the power of the central government at the expense of the states. The *Fletcher v. Peck* decision represented a turning point in American federalism. Until 1810, state legislatures had been generally secure in their legislative authority and political sovereignty. They had reaffirmed this stance by the quick ratification of the Eleventh Amendment in 1793 after the Supreme Court had allowed Georgia to be sued without its consent in the controversial *Chisholm v. Georgia* decision. The Eleventh Amendment guaranteed "state sovereign immunity" and prohibited the general government from dragging a state to federal court. But because *Fletcher v. Peck* involved only individuals, Georgia could not retard the case from moving forward. It was not being sued, but an act by its legislature was at the center of the debate. Now, the Supreme Court had the chance to undermine state authority, something Marshall had been chomping at the bit to do since the 1790s. *Fletcher v. Peck* has since been used as justification in nearly seventy-five Supreme Court decisions invalidating state law.[12] To say it was important is an understatement.

Marshall first dealt with the issue of bribery. While he sympathized with the accusation that the people of Georgia had been swindled, calling it "circumstances most deeply to be deplored," he could not, in his estimation, differentiate between claimants, particularly when as in the case of Fletcher, there appeared to be an honest purchase of land through a verified contract. Plainly, Marshall was not going to let the issue of graft influence his decision. To do so would betray the interests of the "innocents" and create a precedent that future states would use to the detriment of its citizens. Marshall believed that if he were to uphold the nullification of the Yazoo legislation, he would open the door to similar actions by other states across the Union. This was something he could not support, even if the law being nullified was an obvious case of graft.

This may seem to be a principled defense of contract law, but Marshall knew what he was doing. It became clear when he expanded his ruling to include what he considered to be constitutional questions; the most important were, did the Georgia legislature violate Article I, Section 10 of the Constitution, which denied the states the ability of "impairing the Obligation of Contracts" and was the repeal of the Yazoo legislation an ex post facto law and bill of attainder? Marshall answered yes to each. The original titleholders to the Yazoo lands were deprived of their property without a trial (bill of attainder) through legislation that retroactively (ex post facto) nullified their contracts (impairing the obligation of contracts). Thus, the

Georgia law revoking the original sale of the land was unconstitutional. It did not matter that the repeal of the Yazoo claims was the rightful remedy for such an egregious and blatant example of corruption. Marshall and the Supreme Court had essentially found fraud to be constitutional by declaring a state law unconstitutional. He explained why:

> Whatever respect might have been felt for the state sovereignties, it is not to be disguised that the framers of the constitution viewed, with some apprehension, the violent acts which might grow out of the feelings of the moment; and that the people of the United States, in adopting this instrument, have manifested a determination to shield themselves and their property from the effects of those sudden and strong passions to which men are exposed. The restrictions on the legislative power of the states are obviously founded on this sentiment; and the constitution of the United States contains what may be deemed a bill of rights for the people of each state.[13]

This was creative construction. Marshall was interpreting the Constitution and the Philadelphia Convention (which he did not attend) in the way he wanted it to be understood. The "restrictions on the legislative power of the states" were inserted into the document because the states had already "granted" or prohibited those powers to the general government. Additionally, by expanding the contract clause to cover not only private contracts between individuals, but public contracts between sovereign political entities and private parties, Marshall was distorting the original intent of the language. The "obligation of contracts" clause was meant to be a safeguard against paper money and the evils of inflation and state government default. This is why the clause followed the prohibition on states making "any Thing but gold and silver Coin a tender in Payment of Debts...." Virtually anyone who discussed the clause in either the Philadelphia Convention or the state ratifying conventions related it to that issue alone, including Patrick Henry, George

Mason, William Grayson, and Edmund Randolph in the same Virginia Ratifying Convention that Marshall attended.

It must be said that Marshall did not come up with this broad interpretation of the contract clause on his own. Hamilton was intervening from the afterlife. In 1795, Hamilton wrote a brief opinion on the contract clause of the Constitution in regard to the Yazoo scandal. He was questioned about its meaning by Charles Pinckney, the American minister to Spain, who was busy solidifying a treaty between the Spanish crown and the United States. Spanish claims to the Yazoo lands were under discussion, and Pinckney wanted to gather Hamilton's thoughts on the issue. In typical form, Hamilton stressed an expanded view of federal power:

> In addition to these general considerations, placing the revocation in a very unfavourable light, the constitution of the United States, article first, section tenth, declares that no state shall pass a law impairing the obligations of contract. This must be equivalent to saying, no state shall pass a law revoking, invalidating, or altering a contract. Every grant from one to another, whether the grantor be a state or an individual, is virtually a contract that the grantee shall hold and enjoy the thing granted against the grantor, and his representatives. It, therefore, appears to me, *that taking the terms of the constitution in their large sense, and giving them effect according to the general spirit and policy of the provisions*, the revocation of the grant by the act of the legislature of Georgia, may justly be considered as contrary to the constitution of the United States, and, therefore null; and that the courts of the United States, in cases within their jurisdiction, will be likely to pronounce it so [emphasis added].[14]

Marshall couldn't have written it better himself. Marshall was rarely original in his decisions, and this was not the first or the last time he used Hamilton's machinations on the Constitution to defend his brand of judicial activism, nor would it be the last time the Marshall court waged a legal war against state power. They were only getting started. While both *Marbury v. Madison* and *Fletcher v. Peck* fundamentally changed the nature of the Constitution and the relationship between the federal government and the states, two later decisions by the Marshall court would further codify Hamilton's opinions on state power and federal supremacy, in essence allowing the long-dead secretary of the treasury to continue screwing up America from his nearly two-decade dirt nap.

CHAPTER NINE

MARSHALL CODIFIES IMPLIED POWERS

H amilton's First Bank of the United States failed to get re-chartered in a highly politicized vote in 1811. Interestingly, James Madison, now president, and Albert Gallatin, now secretary of the treasury, had reversed course on the constitutionality of a central bank and favored renewing the institution for another twenty years. Debate in Congress was as spirited as it was partisan. After the bill to re-charter the bank sat deadlocked in a 17-17 tie in the United States Senate, Vice President George Clinton, longtime Hamilton foe and erstwhile leading opponent of the Constitution in New York, cast the deciding vote against renewal.

His short speech against the bank echoed the arguments Madison and Jefferson had made against the bank in 1791. "It cannot be doubted," he said, "but that the Congress may pass all laws necessary and proper for carrying into execution the powers specifically granted to the Government, or to any department or officer thereof; but in doing so the means must be suited and subordinate to the end. The power to create corporations is not expressly granted; it is a high attribute of sovereignty and in its nature not accessorial or derivative by implication, but primary and independent." The bank was unconstitutional from the beginning and should never have been chartered in the first place. Clinton emphatically insisted that implied powers would have "an inevitable tendency to consolidation, and affords just and serious cause of alarm."[1]

Clinton was correct. The entire purpose of Hamilton's legislative program from start to finish had been the consolidation of the states under a "supreme" national government. Neither time nor practice had changed that goal, and one-time foes such as Madison and Gallatin had become willing accomplices in the unconstitutional expansion of central authority. The only thing that had not changed, as Clinton correctly asserted, was the Constitution itself.

Had Hamilton still been alive in 1811, there is no doubt he would have taken up his pen against Clinton and every member of Congress who knocked down his precious bank. His moonlighting as a journalist did much to convince many Americans of the necessity of centralization even if it contradicted his own statements about the Constitution when it was up for ratification. Fortunately for proponents of a central banking system, the War of 1812 made it seem as if a new bank was necessary to secure American finances and independence.

Federal revenue was collected almost exclusively from tariffs in the early nineteenth century. With the British blockade of American ports during the war and the elimination of British trade, the American treasury reached critical lows. It had little money to either fight the war or carry out the necessary functions of government. Government bonds were virtually worthless and New England banks—bitter that the war had been commenced in the first place—refused to lend money to the general government. It was only through the intercession of two wealthy mid-Atlantic merchants, Stephen Girard of Pennsylvania and John Jacob Astor of New York, that the United States government continued to operate. They had invested heavily in government bonds and treasury notes, and because of their hefty financial support for the war, began barking about the necessity of another central banking system.

Both had contact with the Madison administration through Alexander J. Dallas, a wealthy lawyer and merchant about to be sworn in as secretary of the teasury. Dallas sympathized with their call for a Second Bank of the United States, and he began pressuring both Madison and leaders in Congress to draft another bill chartering a new bank. Proponents of a new bank drew up a bill that passed both houses of Congress in 1815, but neither Madison nor Dallas was happy with the language, specifically because it weakened the ability of the new bank to lend the United States government money and because it placed too much control over the institution in private hands.

But what about the Constitution? There was some rumbling in the Congress about the constitutionality of a new bank, but this position never became a serious stumbling block to the establishment of a second bank of the United States. Madison himself dislocated the bank from the Constitution when he vetoed the 1815 bank bill. His veto message included a flippant denial that the bank was unconstitutional, a position he had fervently defended less than twenty-five years prior. "Waiving the question of the constitutional authority of the Legislature to establish an incorporated bank as being precluded in my judgment by repeated recognitions under varied circumstances of the validity of such an institution in acts of the legislative, executive, and judicial branches of the Government, accompanied by indications, in different modes, of a concurrence of the general will of the nation..." Madison vetoed the bill because he thought it was bad legislation, not because it was unconstitutional.[2]

Madison then doubled down on his advocacy for a new bank in his 1815 annual message to Congress. Though Madison wrote the address, a careless reading might lead someone to think Hamilton had prepared it before he died. Gone were Madison's concerns about implied powers and misconstruction. Instead, Madison favored the chartering of a national bank, higher protective tariffs, the creation of a national university, and the construction of roads and canals through the "national authority."[3] Some of these recommendations bore fruit. The Congress quickly went to work on another bank bill and sent it to Madison's desk in April 1816 where he willingly signed it into law on April 10. Without much in the way of congressional opposition to the bill, it would fall on the states to challenge the incorporation of a Second Bank of the United States.[4]

An economic panic in 1819 made the Second Bank of the United States a juicy target for those concerned about its influence on the American economy. They had help. A European economic recovery following the Napoleonic Wars led to rapidly falling American agricultural prices. Cotton and foodstuffs tanked on the open market. The improving European economy also led to higher gold and silver prices thus making both more difficult to acquire, even for central banks. In the meantime, American merchants, farmers, and manufacturers had been lured into the easy credit offered by the Second Bank and had rapidly and foolishly expanded beyond what market forces would allow. This was a classic bubble made possible by government control of the monetary supply and credit requirements. When the bubble burst, the American economy collapsed and American debtors began defaulting on their loans. This spike in unpaid debt put the bank in danger of collapsing. It did not have the resources to pay its own debts.

To stop the bleeding, the bank required local banks to repay their loans to the central bank in specie alone, and it forced all branches to redeem only those bank notes issued by that branch. For example, if someone had a bank note redeemable in gold from the Cincinnati branch and took it to the New York branch for payment, he would be denied and instructed to travel to Cincinnati for relief. As the Panic of 1819 grew and economic misery broadened, many Americans began blaming the Second Bank as the root cause of their misery. After all, it had been sold as a necessity for *preventing* such catastrophe. There was some truth in this as the bank's loose lending policies led to what are now called "malinvestments," but all of that was set aside in favor of a legal argument against the bank. The arguments Madison and Jefferson made against the First Bank of the United States in 1791 would be dusted off and reasserted by opponents of the Second Bank of the United States in 1819.[5]

States reacted to the Second Bank of the United States in various ways. Indiana, Illinois, and Tennessee attempted to block the bank from setting up shop within their borders, while Kentucky and Ohio levied high taxes on the branches, which were designed to drive it out of business. Still other states enacted taxes on the bank in an effort to siphon off some of its extensive profits. Maryland was among that group of states. Its policies were not centered on open hostility to the bank—it did not raise a single objection to the bank on constitutional grounds—but were confined to an effort to raise revenue. This did not sit well with the director of the Baltimore branch of the bank. He refused to pay the tax and instead made a federal case out of the issue, which he hoped would end up in the Supreme Court. His wish came true and Marshall's court perhaps even engaged in collusion with the defense to ensure that constitutional questions would ultimately be decided by the case.

Maryland chose three attorneys to represent the state, the most important being Maryland Attorney General Luther Martin, a brash statesman who had famously opposed the Constitution both at the Philadelphia Convention and in the months leading to ratification in 1788. By 1819, his attitude toward the general government had softened, not because he had become an ardent nationalist, but because he hated Thomas Jefferson. Martin had successfully helped defend former vice president and Hamilton assassin Aaron Burr during his scuffle with the general government over treason charges in 1807, and before that had Supreme Court Justice Samuel Chase acquitted in his impeachment trial in 1805. Both outcomes infuriated Jefferson. Martin was not in good health in 1819. He drank too much and suffered from various physical ailments that ultimately resulted in paralysis, but his newfound devotion to federal legislation may have led to his placement on the defense team. Martin, it was believed, was not going to rock the boat in regard to the constitutionality of the bank even if that is what the people of Maryland and the United States at large wanted. But anyone who believed this would be seriously disappointed.

The United States also chose three men to argue its case. This broke precedent. To this point, the Supreme Court had allowed only two attorneys for each side per case. That was increased to three for what became known as *McCulloch v. Maryland*. Everyone in the general government anticipated this would be one of the most important decisions in the history of the United States, probably because Marshall had leaked the contents of the case and its potential impact to several loose-lipped members of Washington society, including the counsel for the United States, William Pinkney, Daniel Webster, and William Wirt. Pinkney had, in fact, coached Webster on the proper arguments to make in the case through the confidence of good information as to what the court wanted. Thus, when the court began hearing the case in February 1819, it may have been a foregone conclusion how the court would vote. This decision would ultimately codify Hamilton's loose construction of the Constitution and his support for implied powers.[6]

That became apparent when Webster began his arguments for the United States. At this point in his career, Daniel Webster did not have the reputation he would acquire as a United States senator from Massachusetts. He was a good lawyer but a notorious flip-flopper. Webster supported the right of state nullification and secession during the War of 1812 when the interests of New England were being subordinated to the general will, but by 1819 he had become a firm proponent of American nationalism, primarily because it worked well for the people of New England at that point. Webster never ceased to be a New England sectionalist. He hid behind nationalism when that suited and sectionalism when it didn't. Banking and loose construction favored his people in 1819, and so he pursued that policy with vigor.

In what became an almost verbatim recitation of Hamilton's defense of the First Bank to Washington in 1791, Webster emphatically declared that the bank was obviously constitutional if for no other reason than custom and precedent had made it so. This sounded more like Madison in 1815 than Hamilton in 1791, but Webster wasn't done. He defended a liberal reading of the "necessary and proper clause" of the Constitution, the same tactic Hamilton had used in 1791. To Webster, "necessary and proper" meant "*Best* and *most useful* to the end proposed," not "*absolutely* indispensable" as Jefferson had originally claimed. Webster defended the ability of Congress to charter corporations under the faulty reasoning that the ends justified the means. The bank could only be classified as unconstitutional if it was shown "that a bank has no fair connection with the execution of any power or duty of the national government, and that its creation is consequently a manifest usurpation." Put simply, if Congress said it needed the bank, then the bank was constitutional.

Having established to his own satisfaction a justification for a loose interpretation of the necessary and proper clause, Webster then focused on the issue of federal supremacy. Did the state of Maryland have a right to tax a federal institution? No, said Webster, because this violated the supremacy clause of the Constitution. He concluded that:

> Nothing can be plainer than that, if the law of Congress establishing the bank be a constitutional fact, it must have its full and complete effects. Its operations cannot be either defeated or impeded by acts of state legislation. To hold otherwise, would be to declare, that the Congress can only exercise its constitutional powers subject to the controlling discretion, and under the sufferance, of the state governments.[7]

What about the other side? Martin spoke as a learned sage bringing wisdom from the past, in this case the Philadelphia Convention and the state ratifying conventions. His role as a pest during the debate over ratification served him well at this juncture. Martin correctly insisted that loose construction as advanced by Hamilton and now Webster was expressly rejected by both the Philadelphia Convention and the friends of the Constitution in 1788. The Tenth Amendment to the Constitution, which served as a "restrictive" force on "misconstruction," was added to the document to codify the general consensus as to the meaning of federal power when the Constitution was adopted. The power to charter corporations was not one of the specifically enumerated powers granted to the general government by the states. Moreover, Martin used the words of the proponents of the Constitution to defend the right of Maryland to tax the Bank of the United States. "The debates in the State conventions show that the power of State taxation was understood to be absolutely unlimited, except to imposts and tonnage duties. The states would not have adopted the Constitution among any other understanding."[8] This was true. Proponents of the document insisted that every state possessed any power not specifically denied to the states by Article I, Section 10 of the Constitution. That included taxation.

This was one of the few times—if not the only time—that anyone had argued original intent by citing the ratification debates in an argument before the Supreme Court. Martin was plowing new ground, but everyone who followed would leave it fallow, perhaps because it had little impact on the unanimous decision of the court handed down by Marshall on March 6, 1819, just three days after the close of oral arguments. This was a fait accompli, but at least Martin put up a good fight.

Marshall took the opportunity in *McCulloch v. Maryland* to fire both barrels at the Jeffersonian concept of the Union, namely that the Constitution formed a compact between sovereign states with expressly delegated powers.[9] He also addressed the issue of judicial review and again struck at the nullifiers. Marshall concluded that the Supreme Court was the only suitable arena to decide conflicts between the states and the general government. "No tribunal can approach such a question without a deep sense of its importance," Marshall wrote, "and of the awful responsibility involved in its decision. But it must be decided peacefully, or remain a source of hostile legislation, perhaps of hostility of a still more serious nature; and if it is to be so decided, by this tribunal alone can the decision be made." Then for the "obiter dissertation" on constitutional powers: "On the Supreme Court of the United States has the constitution of our country devolved this important duty." Marshall was playing fast and loose with the facts, but he had the floor and an opportunity to double down on the supremacy of the federal court system and its ability to be the final arbiter of all constitutional questions.

Marshall then painted the nationalist interpretation of the Constitution with broad strokes. He intended to conclusively silence those who considered the Constitution a mere compact between states. Here, as in previous decisions, Marshall fabricated a narrative out of thin air, one that would be echoed by every nationalist from his day to ours:

> In discussing this question, the counsel for the State of Maryland [Luther Martin] have deemed it of some importance, in the construction of the constitution, to consider that instrument not as emanating from the people, but as the act of sovereign and independent States. The powers of the general government, it has been said, are delegated by the States, who alone are truly sovereign; and must be exercised in subordination to the States, who alone possess supreme dominion.
>
> It would be difficult to sustain this proposition. The Convention which framed the constitution was indeed elected by the State legislatures. But the instrument, when it came from their hands, was a mere proposal, without obligation, or pretensions to it. It was reported to the then existing Congress of the United States, with a request that it might "be submitted to a Convention of Delegates, chosen in each State by the people thereof, under the recommendation of its Legislature, for their assent and ratification." This mode of proceeding was adopted; and by the Convention, by Congress, and by the State Legislatures, the instrument was submitted to the people. They acted upon it in the only manner in which they can act safely, effectively, and wisely, on such a subject, by assembling in Convention. It is true, they assembled in their several States—and where else should they have assembled? *No political dreamer was ever wild enough to think of breaking down the lines which separate the States, and of compounding the American people into one common mass.* Of consequence, when they act, they act in their States. But the measures they adopt do not, on that account, cease to be the measures of the people themselves, or become the measures of the State governments [emphasis added].

This portion of Marshall's decision is the greatest coup in American political and legal history. In short, Marshall distorted the nature of both the Philadelphia Convention and the state ratifying conventions. His decision is nothing more than a lie, a fairy tale in the same vein as the Brothers Grimm. There were men in the Philadelphia Convention who wanted to abolish the states, Hamilton foremost among them, and who considered the states to be a drag on the American system, but they were out-voted and out-maneuvered. The final draft of the Constitution was voted on by state, not by individual, and expressly declares in Article VII that the document is an agreement (compact) "between the States so ratifying the same." Ratification of the Constitution relied on the decision of nine states while those states that chose not to ratify were regarded as independent republics operating outside of the legal authority of the United States. Certainly, the people of the states in convention, not the state governments, ratified the document, but the states were the agents of the people of the states and not of the Union as a whole as Marshall contends. That was painfully clear in every state convention held across the Union in 1787 and 1788.

Marshall then sought to prove that loose construction and federal supremacy were the only possible interpretations of the document. On one hand, Marshall admitted that the Constitution created a general government of limited, enumerated powers, but "the government of the Union, though limited in powers, is supreme within its sphere of action." This position, Marshall argued, was codified by the supremacy clause of the Constitution. This was, however, an irrelevant argument. Marshall was merely invoking a straw man. No one, not even the most ardent states' rights zealots, contended that the general government did not have supremacy within its delegated powers. But they did believe that when the general government passed laws not "in pursuance thereof," those laws were null and void. Hamilton and virtually every friend of the Constitution made this clear during ratification. Marshall ignored those arguments.

But the biggest tall tales were yet to come. Marshall actually agreed with Martin's assertion that chartering a corporation was not one of the enumerated powers of Congress, but he argued it was not necessary because the Constitution did not specifically *deny* that power either. The Tenth Amendment, which Martin had used in his brief against the bank, did not include the word "expressly" before "delegated." Marshall contended this proved the document allowed for "incidental or implied powers." And in one of the more condescending portions of the opinion, Marshall argued that the Framers purposely wrote the document in vague terms because, "A constitution to contain an accurate detail of all the subdivisions of which its great powers will admit, and of all the means by which they may be carried into execution, would partake of a legal code, and could scarcely be embraced by the human mind. It would probably never be understood by the public." Thus, the only logical takeaway from the Philadelphia Convention was that the Constitution was little more than a great outline, "Its important objects designated, and the minor ingredients which compose those objects...deduced from the nature of the objects themselves." He then wove a fanciful tale about the drafting of the instrument. "That this idea was entertained by the framers of the American constitution, is not only to be inferred from the nature of the instrument, but from the language." Any other conclusion would "prevent its receiving a fair and just interpretation.... [W]e must never forget that it is a constitution we are expounding."

Virtually everything Marshall said in this portion of the opinion was false. It was true that the Congress omitted the word "expressly" from the test of the Tenth Amendment, but that was because the members of Congress deemed it unnecessary, not unimportant or too restrictive. "Delegated" and "expressly delegated" carried the same meaning. This was a crafty twisting of words by Marshall. During the state ratifying conventions, the proponents of the Constitution, Marshall among them, insisted that the document would never be at the mercy of implied powers. Additionally, Marshall's claim that the Constitution should be interpreted by the "language" of the document and from inference "from the nature of the instrument" opened the door to a "textual" construction that later became the useful tool of all loose constructionists. Madison insisted late in life that the ratification conventions, not the Philadelphia Convention or the text of the document, "gave it all the validity and authority it possesses."[10] The text of the document had to be placed within the context of original intent, and that intent could only be found in the hundreds of speeches, pamphlets, and public expositions by the friends of the document while it was in the process of ratification.

Marshall summarized his support for loose construction by stressing that the Constitution, "Was intended to endure for ages to come, and, consequently, to be adapted to the various crises of human affairs. To have prescribed the means by which government should in all future time, execute its powers, would have been to change, entirely, the character of the instrument, and give it the properties of a legal code." Marshall foreshadowed every modern argument against so-called strict construction. He justified his opinion by stating, "To have declared that the best means shall not be used, but those alone without which the power given would be nugatory, would have been to deprive the legislature of the capacity to avail itself of experience, to exercise its reason, and to accommodate its legislation to circumstances." Marshall, then, believed that strict construction would limit the ability of the general government to adapt, but this is simply not true. The Constitution can be amended, and the states, as the closest political instruments of the people, had unlimited power to adapt "to the various crises of human affairs."

As for the power to charter a bank, Marshall fell back on Hamilton's exposition of the "necessary and proper clause." Marshall rehashed the Hamiltonian position that the clause had been added to the Constitution "to remove all doubts respecting the right [of Congress] to legislate on that vast mass of incidental powers which must be involved in the constitution, if that instrument not be a splendid bauble." Translation: to Marshall and Hamilton, the necessary and proper clause was the "you can do anything you want" clause. This was not the way proponents of the Constitution sold the document to the states, and though Marshall knew it, he saw continued agitation by strict constructionists undermining the necessity of a strong "national"—not "federal"—government.

Marshall's exclamation point on the issue closely mirrored Hamilton's conclusion in his defense of the bank in 1791:

> But we think the sound construction of the constitution must allow the national legislature that discretion, with respect to the means by which the powers it confers are to be carried into execution, which will enable that body to perform the high duties assigned to it, in the manner most beneficial to the people. *Let the end be legitimate, let it be within the scope of the constitution, and all means which are appropriate, which are plainly adapted to that end, which are not prohibited, but consist with the letter and spirit of the constitution, are constitutional* [emphasis added].

Reaction to the decision was mixed. Only the leading Federalist newspapers of New England supported it enthusiastically. Other newspapers, such as the official organ of the Jefferson, Madison, and James Monroe administrations, the *National Intelligencer,* were lukewarm in support. In contrast, opposition to *McCulloch v. Maryland* from a group of men known as the Richmond Junto was swift and decisive. Led by William Brockenbrough and Spencer Roane, the Junto sliced apart Marshall's nationalism through carefully reasoned and highly original essays under the pseudonyms "Amphictyon" and "Hampden" respectively. Jefferson and Madison considered Brockenbrough and Roane to be longtime and enthusiastic allies. Roane, in fact, would have been appointed to the Supreme Court had Adams not selected Marshall for chief justice shortly before he left office. Brockenbrough was a Richmond judge and Roane was chief justice on the Virginia Court of Appeals, the highest court in the state. Both Roane and Marshall had studied under George Wythe at the College of William and Mary. Their paths crossed several times throughout their careers but they shared little in common other than their native soil.

The Amphictyon essays ran in the *Richmond Enquirer* in March and April 1819. The first challenged Marshall's distortion of the nature of the Union. Brockenbrough wrote that Marshall delivered two blows to the principles of states' rights in the *McCulloch v. Maryland* decision:

> The first is the denial that the powers of the federal government were delegated by the states; and the second is, that the grant of powers to that government, and particularly the grant of powers "necessary and proper" to carry the other powers into effect, ought to be construed in a liberal, rather than a restricted sense. Both of these principles tend directly to consolidation of the states, and to strip them of some of the most important attributes of their sovereignty. If the Congress of the United States should think proper to legislate to the full extent, upon the principles now adjudicated by the supreme court, it is difficult to say how small would be the remnant of power left in the hands of the state authorities.

Brockenbrough argued that each position could conclusively be proven incorrect. Like Jefferson, Brockenbrough considered Marshall's ruminations on the Constitution to be little more than the obiter ramblings of one man traveling "out of the record" for his delegated task. The decision was, Brockenbrough contended, "not more binding or obligatory than the opinion of any other six intelligent members of the community." If the court continued down this path, Brockenbrough saw no hope for real liberty in America, calling it a "fatal consequence to the rights and freedom of the people of the states." He considered the states to be the only "sentinels of the public liberty" and "the protectors of their own rights." The end result would be tyranny. "Every government, which has ever yet been established, feels a disposition to increase its own powers. Without the restraints which are imposed by an enlightened public opinion, this tendency will inevitably conduct the freest government to the exercise of tyrannic power. If the right of resistance be denied, or taken away, despotism inevitably follows."[11]

Roane's Hampden essays followed in the *Richmond Enquirer* in June 1819. Roane possessed an effective and forthright pen. His arguments were concise and appealing, and while they echoed much of what Brocken-brough wrote earlier in the year, he had several nuggets that provided those champions of real federalism with ammunition in their struggle against unconstitutional usurpations of power. "[T]he Supreme Court," he wrote, "has erroneously decided the actual question depending before it: that it has gone far beyond that question, and in an extra-judicial manner, estab-lished an *abstract* doctrine: that they have established it in terms so loose and general, as to give Congress an unbounded authority, and enable them to shake off the limits imposed on them by the Constitution...." Emascu-late the states, and Roane saw no possible method of resistance to illegal acts of the general government. "The people of this vast country when their State legislatures are put aside, will be so sparse and diluted, that they cannot make any effectual head against an invasion of their rights. The triumph over our liberties will be consequently easy and complete. Noth-ing can arrest this calamity, but a conviction of the danger being brought home to the minds of the people."[12]

Batting cleanup for the opposition was another member of the Rich-mond Junto, John Taylor of Caroline. Taylor was without question the most brilliant of the Junto. Taylor had twice served in the United States Senate by 1819 but preferred his life as a planter to public office. He was the most Jeffersonian of the Jeffersonians, a disinterested statesman concerned with the perils of excessive federal overreach. He should be counted among the greatest political philosophers in American history. His several books on agriculture, politics, and government codified the Jeffersonian arguments of real federalism (meaning strict construction), the agrarian political order, and distrust for the fusion of government and finance.

In 1820, Taylor published *Construction Construed and Constitu-tions Vindicated*. He intended the book to be the final say in the *McCull-och v. Maryland* dispute, at least from the opposition. Newspaperman Thomas Ritchie—perhaps the most powerful political voice in Virginia due to his widely read *Richmond Enquirer*—wrote in the introduction that the Bank of the United State had "been justified by the supreme court of the United States, on *principles* so bold and alarming that no man who loves the constitution can fold his arms in apathy upon the subject." In his mind, Marshall's decision could only be understood as "calculated to give the tone to an acquiescent people, to change the whole face of our government, and to generate a thousand measures, which the framers of the constitution never anticipated." The maintenance of the proper division of federal and state power offered the only protection for the American people from both foreign and domestic disturbance. Consolidation would destroy liberty; disunion would destroy peace. In the face of such danger, neither he nor Taylor could stay silent as the general government ran roughshod over the states.[13]

Taylor focused most of his energy on proving that the general government had been created by the people of the states, not the "people" in the aggregate as Marshall contended in his decision, and that implied powers were never considered to be a legitimate exercise of federal authority. "The plural 'states' rejects the idea, that the people of all the states considered themselves as one state. The word 'united' is an averment of pre-existing social compacts, called states; and these consisted of the people of each separate state. It admits the existence of political societies able to contract with each other, and who had previously contracted. And the words "more perfect union" far from implying that the old parties to the old union were superseded by new parties, evidently mean, that these same old parties were about to amend their old union."[14] This is a theme Taylor expounded in earlier works, one that will be discussed in a later chapter, but was used in this case to emphasize Marshall's creative use of language.

Taylor considered the "necessary and proper clause" defense of the bank to be little more than sly sophistry at best and a lie at worst. He had consistently maintained this position during his entire life. Taylor wrote that the "necessary and proper clause" merely limited "the legislative power of congress to laws necessary and proper for executing the *delegated* powers, and bestow no authority to assume powers *not delegated*." As a result, "Congress have no power to enact laws 'necessary and proper' for 'carrying into execution' the powers reserved to the states, as their legislative powers are limited to the *foregoing* or delegated powers; and in cases concerning which congress have no power of legis-lation, the federal courts have no jurisdiction."[15] Taylor was making a valid point, one that had been highlighted in almost every speech in favor of the "necessary and proper clause" during the ratifying conventions. Hamilton moved the argument in a different direction in 1791 and both Webster and Marshall ran with it in 1819 to the general destruction of original intent.

Marshall's opinion in *McCulloch v. Maryland* channeled Webster, who channeled Hamilton. There was nothing original about it, but it became the standard decision in cases involving disputes between federal and state powers and more importantly on issues involving the delegated or granted powers of the United States general government. Marshall made loose construction the *standard* interpretation of the Constitution through this decision and forever relegated strict construction to a long lost fringe "theory" of government. That, of course, was turning history on its head, but no matter. The Supreme Court made it so and the American government and the Constitution have forever been cursed by the ghost of *McCulloch v. Maryland*.

CHAPTER TEN

THE MARSHALL COURT
AND THE STATES

Marshall's shredding of the Constitution as ratified would not have been possible without the Judiciary Act of 1789. Section 25 of that law altered the nature of the relationship between the central government and the states. The Marshall court used it to its advantage in its quest for federal supremacy. There were voices against it in the First Congress, but the real outcry came from what was known as the Richmond Junto, a group of pure constitutionalists who for nearly thirty years held federal representatives accountable for their unconstitutional actions. These men were a refreshing departure from the headlong rush into Hamilton's brand of illegal nationalism, but the story of Marshall's usurpation of state power began in the First Congress.

The Senate first proposed what became known as the Judiciary Act of 1789 on June 12. Because Senate sessions were closed to the public until 1795, very little information surrounding the debates exists. It passed by a vote of 14–6 just five days later, making it appear to have sailed through. Senator William Maclay of Pennsylvania opposed the bill, both in its original form and in the version that the House sent back to the Senate in September. His reasoning never changed. Maclay wrote in his journal that he believed very few cases would go before the federal courts because, "The mass of cases would remain with the State judges." But he also considered it to be a "vile law system, calculated for expense and with a design to draw all law business into the Federal courts. The Constitution," he wrote, "is designed to swallow all the State Constitutions by degrees and thus to swallow, by degrees, all the State judiciaries."[1]

The House took up the bill in August. Samuel Livermore of New Hampshire argued that the Judiciary Act would create confusion and hostility toward the general government in the states and reasoned that the bill would establish "a Government within a Government, and one must prevail upon the ruin of the other." To Livermore, the establishment of district courts would unnecessarily force people to be dragged before two courts for the same offense. He said, "There is already in each State a system of jurisprudence, congenial to the wishes of its citizens" and therefore he insisted that another layer of courts would be both unwise and expensive.[2] William Loughton Smith of South Carolina agreed, and insisted that not only was an extensive federal court system unwise, he reasoned that "this constant control of the Supreme Federal Court over the adjudication of the State courts, would dissatisfy the people, and weaken the importance and authority of State judges. Nay, more, it would lessen their respectability in the eyes of the people, even in causes which properly appertain to the State jurisdictions; because the people, being accustomed to see their decrees overhauled and annulled by a superior tribunal, would soon learn to form an irreverent opinion of their importance and abilities." Smith urged his fellow congressmen, "to draw a broad line of distinction" between the state and federal court systems, "to assign clearly to each its precise limits, and to prevent a clashing or interference between them."[3] That didn't happen.

Smith understood the importance of the issue, and his prognostications would later come true. Section 25 of the Judiciary Act allowed for direct appeal of state court decisions to the Supreme Court under a writ of error if a case could be made that the state law in question violated the United States Constitution. This section, more than any other provision of the bill, disrupted the nature of the Union. Proponents of the bill reasoned that it would only be used in extreme circumstances, but as Smith knew before the act passed into law, eventually people would bypass the state courts by seeking relief in federal court for issues that were plainly outside of its jurisdiction. Section 25 established "federal supremacy" beyond the scope of the ratifiers' promises in 1787 and 1788. Some of those men sat in the First Congress, including the author of the Judiciary Act, future Supreme Court Chief Justice Oliver Ellsworth.

Ellsworth was a leading proponent of the Constitution in Connecticut during ratification. Together with Roger Sherman, Ellsworth penned a letter to Governor Samuel Huntington on September 26, 1787, which forcefully argued that the powers of the general government were specifically defined by Article I, Section 8. Ellsworth published a series of essays just over two months later under the pseudonym "A Landholder" designed to swing votes for ratification in Connecticut. His December 10, 1787 piece was intended to refute several objections made to the Constitution by George Mason of Virginia, which included a fear that, "The judiciary of the United States is so constructed and extended as to absorb and destroy the judiciaries of the several states...." Ellsworth swore this would never happen. The judicial power, he wrote, "extends only to objects and cases specified, and wherein the national peace or rights or the harmony of the states are concerned...."[4]

He then seemingly contradicted himself. During the Connecticut Ratifying Convention in January 1788, Ellsworth contended that the federal courts could invalidate both federal and state law if either were to "go beyond their limits" and make a law which "the Constitution does not authorize" or "which is a usurpation upon the general government...."[5] Clearly the Judiciary Act of 1789 more closely resembled the views of Ellsworth at the January Connecticut Ratifying Convention than Ellsworth the "Landholder" just one month prior. His speeches in the ratifying convention were widely printed, so Ellsworth was not trying to run from his positions. But his statements in January reflected the fear of every opponent of the Constitution should the document be ratified. Section 25 of the Judiciary Act merely codified federal judicial supremacy in the manner Maclay predicted, the way Smith insisted it would be applied, and the way opponents of the Constitution warned the federal courts would operate.

Two landmark Supreme Court decisions challenging the legality of Section 25 of the Judiciary Act indirectly bookended *McCulloch v. Maryland*: *Martin v. Hunter's Lessee* in 1816 and *Cohens v. Virginia* in 1821. Spencer Roane and the Richmond Junto led the effort to undermine federal power in both cases. Marshall uncharacteristically recused himself from the former but issued the majority opinion in the latter. No matter. Marshall's court was squarely in line with his judicial philosophy, and Marshall himself could not have written a more sweeping decision than the one Associate Justice Joseph Story penned in *Martin v. Hunter's Lessee*.

Martin v. Hunter's Lessee centered on a decades-old land dispute. In 1781, Thomas Fairfax, Sixth Lord Fairfax of Cameron, died and deeded his substantial Northern Virginia landholdings, arguably the best land in the region, to his nephew, Denny Fairfax. Thomas Fairfax was a loyalist who fled Virginia during the American War for Independence and Denny Fairfax remained a British citizen. The following year, the Virginia House of Delegates passed a confiscatory statute voiding the transfer of all property to foreign aliens. This was intended to block loyalists from holding onto property after the war, most significantly Denny Fairfax. The state of Virginia became the legal property holder of confiscated land and proceeded to sell or grant large tracts to those who had supported the patriot cause.

David Hunter of Winchester, Virginia received 788 acres of Lord Fairfax's estate. He filed a lawsuit in county court to legally oust Denny Fairfax. This should have been a slam-dunk, but surprisingly the county court decided against him. Hunter then appealed the decision to the Virginia Court of Appeals, which reversed the lower court's decision. This appeared to end the squabble, but the 1783 Treaty of Paris complicated the issue. According to the treaty, loyalist property had to be both returned and respected by American legal and political institutions, thus essentially invalidating all confiscation acts passed during the war, including the one that seized Fairfax's land. The case languished in Virginia courts for another two decades as Jay's Treaty between Great Britain and the United States in 1794 reaffirmed the property provisions of the Treaty of Paris while the state of Virginia refused to budge.

The case finally landed in the Supreme Court in 1813 as *Fairfax's Devisee v. Hunter's Lessee*. In a decision stuffed with pedantic legal jargon, Judge Story, serving in place of the recused Marshall, sided with Denny Fairfax by asserting that due to the supremacy clause of Article VI of the Constitution, Virginia had to abide by the terms of Jay's Treaty, thus rendering the Court of Appeals decision unconstitutional. Story had essentially struck down a state law and implicitly reduced Virginia to an administrative subdivision of the United States. That was the point. Story was as much a nationalist as Marshall, and he took any and all opportunity to enlarge the power and influence of the general government at the expense of the states.

The Virginia Court of Appeals countered by ignoring the ruling and denying that Marshall had the authority to issue a writ of mandamus to execute its order. It contended that it was not required to abide by Supreme Court decisions that traveled outside the court's delegated jurisdiction. This was judicial nullification of both a federal court decision and Section 25 of the Judiciary Act. Led by Roane, the Court of Appeals explained its position: "The appellate power of the Supreme Court of the United States does not extend to this court, under a sound construction of the Constitution of the United States; that so much of the 25th section of the act of Congress...is not in pursuance of the Constitution of the United States...and that obedience to its mandate be declined by this court."[6] The other justices on the Court of Appeals wrote separate opinions that echoed Roane. Judge William H. Cabell, a brilliant legal scholar, statesman, former governor of Virginia, and one-time political protégé of Jefferson, wrote that "one court cannot be correctly said to be superior to another, unless both of them belong to the same sovereignty.... The courts of the United States, therefore, belonging to one sovereignty, cannot be appellate courts in relation to the state courts, which belong to a different sovereignty."[7] These statements reinforced the original understanding of the Constitution and the federal judiciary, particularly the way in which the Constitution was sold to Virginia during ratification, notably by John Marshall himself. Jefferson and Madison couldn't have said it better in 1798.

This direct attack on the federal court system did not go unnoticed. The Supreme Court quickly took up the case again in early 1816 under a writ of error, this time as *Martin v. Hunter's Lessee*. Lead council for the United States, Walter Jones (the same Walter Jones who defended Maryland in *McCulloch v. Maryland* in 1819!), contended that the government under the Constitution "was not a mere confederacy.... In its legislative, executive, and judicial authorities, it is a national government, to every purpose, within the scope of the objects enumerated in the Constitution." This rendered the state courts inferior to the federal court system, meaning "the state courts are to adjudicate under the supreme law of the land, as a rule binding upon them." Therefore, no state court could invalidate a federal ruling.[8]

The defense cried foul and claimed that not only were both the writ of error and writ of mandamus completely illegal, the entire federal position rested on a creative version of history. Samuel Dexter of Massachusetts, the former Federalist secretary of war in the John Adams administration and a member of the secessionist Essex Junto faction of New England in 1803, made a compelling case for states' rights. Dexter did not share the same views as Roane or the Richmond Junto—he was much more of a nationalist—but he did believe that the general government could abuse its authority. The Judiciary Act was a perfect example. He called it "neither constitutionally nor politically adapted to enforce the powers of the national courts in a pacific and amicable manner." Dexter argued that disunion was a much greater threat than centralization to peace and stability, but he would "not strain and break the constitution in order to assert the [constitutional powers of the national government]."[9] This was the softer side of decentralization, a mild form of federalism to which neither Hamilton, Marshall, nor Story subscribed.

The only consistent dissent on the Marshall court flowed from the pen of Jefferson appointee William Johnson, and even he at times, to Jefferson's consternation, sided with Marshall.

Story listened, but perhaps he took Marshall's advice to a young John Bannister Gibson: "Look a lawyer straight in the eyes for two hours and [do] not hear a damned word he says," for Story had already made up his mind before oral arguments began.[10] An unsubstantiated rumor also floated about that Marshall wrote the opinion and gave it to Story to deliver. There were noticeable similarities between Story's decision in *Martin v. Hunter's Lessee* and Marshall's in *McCulloch v. Maryland* three years later. This could be mere coincidence or it could be that though Marshall recused himself from the case, he wanted to drive home his position on "national supremacy." Either way, it was a foregone conclusion that the court would again smack down the Virginia Court of Appeals, though this time Story's forty-page opinion would embrace larger constitutional questions than those in the more narrow decision in *Fairfax's Devisee v. Hunter's Lessee*.

Story understood the gravity of the case. If Virginia was correct, then the power of the federal judiciary would be greatly reduced. Perhaps a more accurate term would be *emasculated*. He was not going to let that happen, even if it meant making up history as he went. For Story, this would be par for the course, particularly with respect to his later writings. The Marshall court had made great strides in codifying Hamilton's vision of a strong central government, and in 1816 Story was the guardian of that legacy.

Story opened by writing that, "The constitution of the United States was ordained and established, not by the states in their sovereign capacities, but emphatically, as the preamble of the constitution declares, by 'the people of the United States.'" This is the same logic Marshall used in *McCulloch v. Maryland*. Story then admitted that the states' sovereign powers "remained unaltered and unimpaired," but with the qualification "except so far as they were granted to the government of the United States." That was the key, for then Story advanced the common "textual" narrative of the Constitution that Marshall would later use as the backbone of his arguments in favor of loose construction. Story continued, "this instrument, like every other grant, is to have a reasonable construction, according to the import of its terms; and where a power is expressly given in general terms, it is not to be restrained to particular cases, unless that construction grow out of the context expressly, or by necessary implication. The words are to be taken in their natural and obvious sense, and not in a sense unreasonably restricted or enlarged." Story wrapped up his introduction with a rhetorical flourish. In language that Marshall would echo three years later, Story insisted that:

> The constitution unavoidably deals in general language. It did not suit the purposes of the people, in framing this great charter of our liberties, to provide for minute specifications of its powers, or to declare the means by which those powers should be carried into execution. It was foreseen that this would be a perilous and difficult, if not an impracticable, task. The instrument was not intended to provide merely for the exigencies of a few years, but was to endure through a long lapse of ages, the events of which were locked up in the inscrutable purposes of Providence. It could not be foreseen what new changes and modifications of power might be indispensable to effectuate the general objects of the charter; and restrictions and specifications, which, at the present, might seem salutary, might, in the end, prove the overthrow of the system itself. Hence its powers are expressed in general terms, leaving to the legislature, from time to time, to adopt its own means to effectuate legitimate objects, and to mould and model the exercise of its powers, as its own wisdom, and the public interests, should require.

Progressives everywhere would sing hosannas to Story's ingenious warping of original intent, for it opened the door to every unconstitutional legislative program of the nineteenth and twentieth centuries. This was the same argument used by both Hamilton and Marshall to enlarge the powers under the "necessary and proper clause." Story used it to expand the meaning of the "supremacy clause." He understood that it was inevitable that "cases within the judicial cognizance of the United States" would be heard in state court, but the supremacy clause made it clear that state judges would be bound to decide not "merely according to the laws or constitution of the state, but according to the constitution, laws and treaties of the United States—'the supreme law of the land.'" Story was not denying that the states had powers; he was denying that the states had the ability to use those powers to check unconstitutional acts by the general government. Story reasoned that because the Constitution operated on the states "in their corporate capacities" by stripping or annulling their sovereignty, it became clear through any reasonable construction that the federal government was "supreme." What Story feared most were "state attachments, state prejudices, state jealousies, and state interests" obstructing or controlling "the regular administration of justice." Story's reduction of the states to "corporations" sounded a lot like Hamilton in 1787, which was typical nationalist fare, but now it had the weight of the Supreme Court behind it.

Yet who measured what constituted "unreasonable" acts of Congress, and who, then, would have "the absolute right of decision, in the last resort...?" Why, the Supreme Court, of course. State courts, Story argued, could have no role in this process because "the necessity of *uniformity* of decision throughout the whole United States, upon all subjects within the purview of the constitution" had to be lodged within the federal court system. If not, the end result would be the fracturing of the Union. Story could find no power giving Virginia the authority to ignore a federal court order or to declare Section 25 of the Judiciary Act to be unconstitutional. In fact, Story wrote that, "the court are of opinion, that the appellate power of the United States does extend to cases pending in the state courts; and that the 25th section of the judiciary act, which authorizes the exercise of this jurisdiction in the specified cases, by a writ of error, is supported by the letter and spirit of the constitution. We find no clause in that instrument which limits this power; and we dare not interpose a limitation where the people have not been disposed to create one."[11]

Story upheld the original decision of the court and invalidated the Virginia confiscation acts. He wrote in 1830 that *Martin v. Hunter's Lessee* "decided the very important question of the *right* of Congress to give the Supreme Court *appellate* jurisdiction over the decisions of *State* Courts on constitutional questions.... I *know*, that, though the Ch[ief] Justice [Marshall] did not sit, he fully concurred in that opinion. On this decision, in effect, rests the whole value and efficacy of our control over the State Courts in their Constitutional decisions. It is *vital* to the government."[12] Yet, contrary to what Story said in 1830, the matter was not settled by *Martin v. Hunter's Lessee*. It continued to fester for several years and was again revisited in the 1821 decision of *Cohens v. Virginia*. This time, Marshall attempted to have the final say. Roane, however, didn't go quietly into the night.

The case of *Cohens v. Virginia* began as a dispute between Virginia and two Maryland citizens over a lottery. P. J. and M. J. Cohen were arrested and sentenced to a substantial fine by a Norfolk, Virginia court for selling lottery tickets within the state of Virginia. The lottery had been approved by the United States Congress and the drawing was to be held in Washington, DC, but lotteries were illegal in Virginia, and so the Cohen brothers were knowingly engaging in criminal activity within the state. They attempted to appeal the decision but were denied because the Virginia legislature had established restrictions on what types of cases could be appealed to higher courts. This case fell under that umbrella. This was an important development. If the Virginia legislature could determine which cases could be heard by the Virginia Court of Appeals, it could also determine which cases could wind up in federal court under Section 25 of the Judiciary Act.

The Cohens' legal team then took an extraordinary step. Rather than simply complying with the decision and paying the hefty fine imposed on their clients, they decided to appeal to the United States Supreme Court. This would bypass the Virginia Court of Appeals and the customary method of due process. At stake were two questions of vast importance.

First, did the Supreme Court have jurisdiction due to the fact that the Virginia Court of Appeals had not yet—and would not—rule on the matter? No one had ever attempted this move in the nearly forty years of American legal history. If the court took up the case, it would be openly attacking the ability of the Virginia legislature to establish rules and regulations for its own judicial system. Second, was the lottery legal? This would be an issue of supremacy. Did federal law trump state law in all cases, even if the federal law openly violated either state law or the state constitution?

Virginia had already prepared for battle. Governor Thomas Mann Randolph (Thomas Jefferson's son-in-law) made the case an issue in his annual address to the legislature. They responded by passing a series of resolutions critical of the Supreme Court that echoed the nullification spirit of 1798. Randolph then appointed Philip Pendleton Barbour and Alexander Smyth to represent the state in court while a legislative committee produced a report denying that the Supreme Court had jurisdiction due the Eleventh Amendment. Virginia argued it could not be sued in court without its consent. Barbour and Smyth were told to confine their arguments to the matter of jurisdiction and if the court decided that it did have jurisdiction in the matter, they were to depart immediately. Barbour and Smyth enthusiastically complied with the mandate.[13]

Both Barbour and Smyth were politically aligned with Roane, Taylor of Caroline, Ritchie, and other members of the Richmond Junto. They firmly believed in the "principles of '98" and an originalist interpretation of the Constitution, one that respected the powers of the states vis-à-vis the general government. The Virginia legislature chose both men to defend the state because of their impeccable republican principles. Barbour was a sitting member of the House of Representatives and would later serve as Speaker of the House and as an associate justice on the United States Supreme Court. Not even Jefferson himself made a better case for state powers than Barbour during his impressive political and legal career, and his oral arguments in the Cohens' case did not disappoint.

Barbour opened by asserting "that the Federal Government is one of limited powers" and as Article III of the Constitution clearly states, the judicial power could only extend to cases "arising under this *constitution, the laws of the United States, and treaties made, or which shall be made, under their authority*." To Barbour, it was evident that the case in question did not meet the criteria expressly stated in Article III. Virginia's prohibition on lotteries and its stringent regulations in regard to legal appeal were not prohibited by Article I, Section 10 of the Constitution, nor were they delegated to the general government by Article I, Section 8. The Supreme Court, then, did not have jurisdiction. This was a precision strike that should have obliterated its target, namely unconstitutional federal judicial encroachment over state powers, but Barbour continued with perhaps the best definition of federalism to ever be placed before a federal court.

Barbour asserted that "a two-fold system of legislation pervades the United States; the one of which I will call *Federal*, the other *municipal*. The first belongs by the constitution of the United States to Congress, and consists of the powers of war, peace, commerce, negotiation, and those general powers, which make up our external relations, together with a few powers of an internal kind, which require uniformity in their operation: the second belongs to the States, and consists of whatever is not included in the first, embracing particularly every thing connected with the internal police and economy of the several States." That is precisely how the Constitution was sold to the states during ratification, but the issue at hand was whether a "municipal" law for Washington, DC applied to every state in the Union.

The general government had both "federal" and "municipal" power in the District of Columbia, but it did not have municipal power in either Virginia or Maryland. Thus, a municipal law for Washington, DC such as paving a road or establishing a lottery, was not applicable to the states. Barbour rightly concluded that "though the laws of Congress, when passed in execution of a federal power, extend over the Union, and being laws of the United States, are a part of the supreme law of the land, yet, a law passed like the one in question, in execution of the power of municipal legislation, extends only so far, as the power under which it was passed—that is, to the boundaries of the District; that, therefore, it is no law of the United States, and consequently not a part of the supreme law of the land." If, however, the general government could extend its municipal powers to every state in the Union, its laws "may be carried to the extent of an *interference with every department of State legislation*; and whenever they shall so interfere, they are to be considered of paramount authority [emphasis added]." This is what every Jeffersonian feared and what every proponent of the Constitution swore would never happen: the creation of a "national" government and the elimination of expressly defined and separate federal and state powers.[14]

Smyth was even more direct: "If you correct the errors of the Courts of Virginia, you either make them Courts of the United States, or you make the Supreme Court of the United States a part of the judiciary of Virginia. The United States can only pronounce the judgment of the United States. Virginia alone can pronounce the judgment of Virginia. Consequently, none but a Virginia Court can correct the errors of a Virginia Court. There is nothing in the constitution that indicates a design to make the State judiciaries subordinate to the judiciary of the United States." The end result, Smyth feared, would be the reduction of the states to mere subdivisions of the federal government and necessitate that all state laws be subject to judicial review in federal court. That was simply not how the federal judiciary was sold to the states. Smyth properly identified what was at risk, the powers of the states and the future of the state courts. He forcefully concluded, "That which is fixed by the constitution, Congress have no power to change. The jurisdiction of the State Courts is fixed by the constitution. It is not a subject for congressional legislation."

Both Barbour and Smyth reiterated that Section 25 of the Judiciary Act was an unconstitutional usurpation of power by the general government and that only Virginia, not Congress, could enlarge or contract its own judicial jurisdiction. If the Supreme Court claimed to have jurisdiction in the case, it was entering into an arena where it had no legal authority. It would be a violation of the constitutional compact and would signal an end to the federal republic forged in 1789, a republic that recognized the sovereignty of the states. As Smyth said, "It would degrade the State governments, and devest [sic] them of every pretension to sovereignty, to determine that they cannot punish offences without their decisions being liable to a re-examination, both as to law and fact, (if Congress please) before the Supreme Court of the United States."[15]

The lead councils for the Cohen brothers, David B. Ogden of New York and William Pinkney (of *McCulloch v. Maryland* fame), simply scoffed at Barbour and Smyth. Ogden proclaimed that the issue of jurisdiction had already been settled by the *Martin v. Hunter's Lessee* case, and besides, he chortled, "We deny, that since the establishment of the national constitution, there is any such thing as a sovereign State, independent of the Union." Then in a bit of nationalist mythmaking he stated, "Every State is limited in its powers by the provisions of the constitution; and whether a State passes those limits, is a question which the people of the Union have not thought fit to trust to the State legislatures or judiciaries, but have conferred it exclusively on this Court."[16] That did not mesh with the historical record, but he had the floor and would use it to help fabricate a narrative that Hamilton first advanced in 1791.

Pinkney followed with a lengthy denunciation of Virginia's legal position. "The supremacy of the national constitution and laws," he bellowed, "is a fundamental principle of the federal government, and would be entirely surrendered to State usurpation, if Congress could not, at its option, invest the Courts of the Union with exclusive jurisdiction over this class of cases, or give those Courts an appellate jurisdiction over them from the decisions of the State tribunals. Every other branch of federal authority might as well be surrendered. To part with this, leaves the Union a mere league or confederacy of States, entirely sovereign and independent." He wrapped up his argument by suggesting that states' rights was a concept "too wild and extravagant" to even be logically contemplated.[17]

This was insane nationalist fear mongering. Neither Barbour nor Smyth contended that the states were entirely independent of the general government. They merely believed, as did most of the leaders in Virginia politics, that the general government could not fabricate powers where none existed and could not dictate to state courts and state legislatures on issues that were not expressly delegated to it by the Constitution. As Barbour said, those powers were confined to "war, peace, commerce, negotiation, and those general powers, which make up our external relations, together with a few powers of an internal kind, which require uniformity in their operation." A lottery did not fall within those powers, nor did the power to assume jurisdiction in a case where it had no authority to act. That was usurpation of the highest order.

Marshall issued his opinion two weeks later. He spent the majority of the time castigating Virginia for its stand against the federal court system and only a small portion on the actual merits of the case, namely if Virginia was correct in arresting and fining the Cohen brothers. This was an opportunity that the sixty-five-year-old nationalist was not going to let go. Virginia had to be publicly reprimanded and forcefully told to cease and desist its attempts to undermine federal power. As in previous cases, Marshall would use some creative history to make his point.

He considered the claim that Virginia could not be sued without its consent and the question of whether the Supreme Court had jurisdiction in the matter to be of primary importance. He classified state opposition to the federal court system as mere "abstract propositions" that would ultimately lead to war should they be pursued by every member of the Union. At stake was the ability of the Supreme Court to act as a final referee in all constitutional questions affecting the United States. Marshall concluded that responsibility had been "assigned to the judicial department" by the "American people." This was only partly true. The "American people" had assigned nothing to the Supreme Court, but here Marshall was doubling down on his assertion in *McCulloch v. Maryland* that the "people" and not the states crafted and ratified the document. And, it was a dubious claim that "judicial review" had been universally accepted or promoted by the ratifying conventions. Obviously that was not the case.

Marshall, however, insisted that, "The people made the constitution, and the people can unmake it. It is the creature of their will, and lives only by their will." In a statement that foreshadowed Abraham Lincoln's arguments against secession just four decades later, Marshall then opined, "But this supreme and irresistible power to make or to unmake, resides only in the whole body of the people; not in any sub-division of them. The attempt of any of the parts to exercise it is usurpation, and ought to be repelled by those to whom the people have delegated their power of repelling it." In one sense, Marshall was correct. The people, through their states, could "unmake" the Constitution. That was clear in Article V, which gave the *states*, not the *people* in the aggregate, the ability to destroy or remake the Constitution through amendments. But it could only occur through the *states*, and only three-fourths of the *states* had to agree, not "the whole body of the people" as Marshall insisted. Such clever dishonesty worked well in a situation where Marshall could not be challenged, but any honest nineteenth-century "fact checker" would have called Marshall out as an opportune liar.

Marshall accomplished other ingenious distortions in this ruling. He narrowly interpreted the Eleventh Amendment, making it virtually impossible moving forward for a state to invoke it to avoid prosecution in federal court. Marshall's reading flew in the face of the amendment's intent, which was to remove all doubt after the *Chisholm v. Georgia* fiasco of 1793 that a state could not be sued in federal court by any foreign citizen, either international or domestic, without its consent—some even later suggested by citizens of its own state without consent. Certainly, this case fit the bill as the Cohen brothers were citizens of Maryland and broke the law in Virginia, but Marshall thought otherwise and outright rejected the claims made by Barbour and Smyth that Virginia was not required to appear in federal court. Marshall also upheld Section 25 of the Judiciary Act by utilizing the same arguments Story voiced in *Martin v. Hunter's Lessee*. Marshall believed in federal judiciary supremacy no matter the situation, and Section 25 allowed the court to maintain that role. Surprisingly, however, Marshall sided with Virginia in the only part of the case where it legally mattered: he affirmed the decision of the municipal court in Virginia and let the fine against the Cohen brothers stand. Yet the damage had already been done. Marshall followed his well-trodden path and adjudicated without explicit power or authority on matters that should have been left alone.

Spencer Roane thought so. He wrote five essays for the *Richmond Enquirer* under the nom de plume Algernon Sidney in late May and early June 1821 challenging Marshall's broad use of federal judicial power. The Supreme Court, he wrote, seems "to have claimed an exemption from the restrictions of the constitution, by the unlimited right they have usurped, to alter the constitution as they please…" and he reminded Marshall and other members of the federal bench that, "The supreme court ought not to have forgotten, that although our general government is a national one as to some purposes, it is a federal one as to others. They ought also to have remembered, that states giving up some of their rights and becoming members of a federal republic, do not, thereby, cease to be sovereign states." This was a direct challenge to the great discoveries Marshall, Story, Pinkney, Webster, and Hamilton had made in their years pontificating on the Constitution. History was not on their side.

These essays were a tour de force of originalist political thought. They addressed and then destroyed every vestige of nationalist constitutional innovations, from the "people created the constitution in the aggregate" myth to the abuse of implied powers and judicial review. Roane prophetically announced that Marshall's expansion of federal judicial power would ruin the states. "It is said," he sniped, "that the government and its laws would be prostrated at the feet of the several states. This argument turns in a circle. If, on the contrary, there is no check existing, on the part of the states, or rather on the part of the constitution, as provided for in favor of the states, all the states in the Union might be demolished by the supreme court. It is just as probable that the government of the United States will usurp more than its due share of power, as that the state will withhold what is its due. It is just as probable that unconstitutional laws will be executed to the injury of the states, as that those which are constitutional will be impeded or resisted."

Roane exposed the real problem with the Marshall court's treatment of the Constitution and federal supremacy: "A federal compact between two parties is a nonentity, if it is whatever one of those parties chooses to make it."[18] To put it another way, Roane reasoned, like Jefferson in the Kentucky Resolutions of 1798, that if the general government had a monopoly on determining the extent of its own powers, it would always side with expansion of those powers at the expense of the states and the Constitution. History has proven Roane correct. He said it better in a letter to James Madison in April 1821: "It is firmly believed, and deeply lamented, that the *late* decision of the Supreme Court of the United States, has sapped the foundations of our Constitution: of that Constitution, which, in its original form, and its subsequent amendments, you were so instrumental in establishing; and which you supported, by the celebrated report, that produced the glorious revolution of 1799. In fact it is believed [sic], that this decision has entirely subverted the principles of that revolution."[19]

Marshall's thirty-five year reign on the Supreme Court did as much to screw up America as Hamilton's brief tenure as secretary of the treasury. In both cases, the promises each made to his respective ratifying conventions contradicted what he did as a participant in the general government. Marshall codified what Hamilton started, and as Roane and the Richmond Junto ably pointed out, the results were the complete subversion of the states to the general will and a willful misconstruction of the Constitution as ratified. America has never recovered.

CHAPTER ELEVEN

JOSEPH STORY AND THE *COMMENTARIES*

No man did more to solidify the nationalist interpretation of the Constitution than Supreme Court Justice Joseph Story. Hamilton provided the kindling, Marshall the spark, and Story stoked the flames into a massive nationalist bonfire that ultimately consumed its foes, including the Constitution as ratified in 1787 and 1788. While Story wrote several important decisions during his thirty-four years on the federal bench, he accomplished most of the damage outside of his official duties on the Supreme Court. Story, who would ultimately become Marshall's right-hand man, was not only a powerful federal judge but also the first Dane Professor of Law at Harvard University and published a massive three-volume comprehensive treatise on the Constitution entitled *Commentaries on the Constitution of the United States*, all while continuing to serve as associate justice. This was and still is unprecedented. Marshall anonymously published editorials defending his decisions throughout his time on the bench, and other judges, even to this day, get onto the speaking circuit as legal celebrities, but Story took that further. His *Commentaries* sold well and along with the more famous *Federalist Papers* became the definitive treatment of the meaning and intent of the Constitution. Additionally, his role as professor of law allowed him to influence generations of legal scholars, lawyers, and judges. Story was attempting to ingrain his legal theories into every prospective lawyer in America. It worked. Story's book royalties, in fact, were almost three times as much as his Supreme Court salary near the end of his life. Everyone read his treatise on the Constitution, making his *Commentaries* a major means by which Story screwed up America.

Story did not begin his career as a nationalist. His republican upbringing led him to support Jeffersonian principles as a young man, even if his principles always had a New England bias. Story was born in Marblehead, Massachusetts, the son of ardent patriot and Sons of Liberty member Dr. Elisha Story. He attended Harvard and after graduating in 1798 studied law for three years before being admitted to the Massachusetts Bar. Story dabbled in poetry and politics. He served in the Massachusetts House of Representatives and for a brief time in the United States Congress. His opposition to Jefferson's controversial embargo was based not on any originalist understanding of federal power but a belief that his constituents were being fleeced by the general government. Story would never be confused for an originalist during his long tenure in public life.

Story, however, showed enough promise as a Jeffersonian to be nominated for the Supreme Court in 1811 by James Madison. He was only thirty-two. In time, Madison would regret his appointment as Story came to represent everything Madison loathed politically, particularly in regard to judicial power. This may have been because Story had not yet defined either his legal or constitutional philosophy. His son, William Wetmore Story, later wrote that his father's understanding of American constitutionalism developed *after* taking his seat on the federal bench. This has long been attributed to Marshall's powerful influence, and as the youngest man in American history to sit on the Supreme Court, there is little doubt that Story was an impressionable justice. W. W. Story disagreed and instead attributed his father's positions to a clearheaded reading of the Constitution and its history: "Upon taking his seat on the Bench, my father devoted himself to this branch of the law, and the result was a cordial adherence to the views of Marshall, whom he considered then and ever afterwards as the expounder of the true principles of the Constitution. Nor did this indicate so much a *change* as a *formation* of opinion, and it is no slight indication of his independence and emancipation from the influence of party, that he resigned, upon careful study and examination into the history and principles of the Constitution, his early prejudices in favor of Mr. Jefferson's abstractions, for the clear and practical doctrines of Marshall."[1] Either way, Story was a wildcard in 1811, but in time he would become as important as Marshall in advancing loose construction, judicial activism, and unrestrained—and unconstitutional—American nationalism.

Story was not a physically imposing figure, but his strong chin, well-proportioned nose, large forehead, and receding hairline gave him the look of a serious man. When highlighted by the small circular spectacles that often adorned his face and the long, combed-back white locks that marked his later years, Story became the perfect caricature of a federal judge or college professor. Whereas Marshall was crass and slovenly, Story presented refinement and manners. His students loved and respected him, as did his legal adversaries. Even Philip Barbour, the staunch old Republican from the Richmond Junto who opposed Story on virtually every issue, struck up a warm friendship with the Yankee judge when the two served on the court together.

What Story lacked in physical appearance he made up for in intellect. He had a sharp mind and was a formidable adversary both as a lawyer and political theorist. But like John Marshall, Story suffered from historical amnesia. His view of the founding period, in particular the writing and ratification of the Constitution, was distorted by a desire to apply the principles of national supremacy to the length and breadth of the American experience. Story manufactured an image of the American founding and American government that did not match the historical record. This makes him dangerous. Conservatives have generally viewed Story's *Commentaries* as an anchor text on the Constitution. His fusion of natural law with the common law tradition of the day coupled with his obvious admiration for the ruminations of British Conservative Edmund Burke have led many Americans on the right to pore over his work for legal validation of their position. For example, former Attorney General and Ronald Reagan Distinguished Fellow Emeritus at The Heritage Foundation Edwin Meese called Joseph Story "a champion of originalist thought." This is a mistake. Story was a textualist, not an originalist. Marshall and Story feared the effect men like Jefferson would have on the fledgling Union. In their minds, the idea of states' rights was not only historically wrong, it would lead to disunion and war.

A cursory review of history would seem to support their claim. States' rights led to the War Between the States, or so it is asserted. National solutions were necessary to maintain continuity and order, and states' rights became a fly in the ointment, the loose bolt in the flywheel that threatened to tear apart the Union into a thousand pieces. But what if this is history turned on its head? What if historians—even conservative fellows like Marshall and Story—have unknowingly followed the Marxist sin of reading history in reverse and finding convenient boogeymen to saddle with the burden of history? What if the great lie of national supremacy and implied powers that began with Hamilton in 1791 and was advanced by John Marshall and his court and Joseph Story and his *Commentaries* was *the* leading factor in American political discord? What if *nationalism* and not states' rights led to the destruction of the Union in 1861 and the resulting political misery of the last 150 years? Story's ingenious though incorrect reading of American history in reverse, of infusing his advocacy for a national identity into American constitutional law, has helped consolidate the "nationalist myth" in American history. It has not always been so, and Story knew it. His *Commentaries* were expressly intended to drive a stake through the heart of the Jeffersonian republican view of American government, a view buttressed by the American experience of independence, the founding of the Union, and the eventual ratification of the Constitution. Like Hamilton and Marshall, Story lied.

Story wrote in his introduction to the *Commentaries* that he did not intend to present any "novel views, and novel constructions of the Constitution..." nor did he have "the ambition to be the author of any new plan of interpreting the theory of the Constitution, or of enlarging or narrowing its powers by ingenious subtleties and learned doubts."[2] This would be true if Story's musings on the Constitution were not born from Hamilton and Marshall's nifty distortion of the document. Implied powers and national supremacy had become part of the American legal lexicon and Story gave them historical potency, even though they resulted from willful deception. This became evident in the first volume.

Story's summary of the founding of the British North American colonies was fairly accurate, that is until he began expounding on the nature of the "union" created during the American War for Independence. Story conceded that the colonies "had no direct political connexion with each other..." with each "in a limited sense...sovereign within its own territory." They had independent legislatures and could not pass any law or privilege that affected any other colony in North America. But then Story concocted a striking myth of American nationalism. These independent colonies somehow comprised "one people." "[A]-lthough the colonies were independent of each other in respect to their domestic concerns, they were not wholly alien to each other. On the contrary, they were fellow subjects, and for many purposes one people." If this was true, then every bit of growling by the states' rights Jeffersonians against national supremacy suffered from insufficient historical evidence. If Americans were "one people," then national supremacy was an extension of the American experience born during the colonial period when every American was a common subject of the king of Great Britain.[3]

Story took this a step further. He concluded that the people of the colonies formed the First and Second Continental Congresses, not through their respective colonies, but as "one people" with the "de facto and de jure" sovereign authority of a "supreme" governing body. In one stroke of the pen, Story obliterated colonial lines and discovered the origins of the national supremacy of his day. Those rascally states' rights partisans had been lying to their constituents the entire time. To Story, the "union" predated the American War for Independence, and that "union" was of people, not states. Story, however, also contradicted his own claim of popular national supremacy just a few sentences later. He wrote that the voting in this new national assembly would be conducted by colony, not delegate, meaning that each colony had one equal vote no matter how many men it sent to Philadelphia.[4] This obliterated his claim that the Continental Congress somehow represented the people and not the colonies and later states, but Story knew once he created his nationalist narrative that he had to run with it even if the evidence worked against his conclusions.

Story then doubled down on his nationalist myth of the American founding. "In the first place," he dreamed, "antecedent to the Declaration of Independence, none of the colonies were, or pretended to be sovereign states, in the sense, in which the term 'sovereign' is sometimes applied to states." Story decided that, "Strictly speaking, in our republican forms of government, the absolute sovereignty of the nation is in the people of the nation; and the residuary sovereignty of each state, not granted to any of its public functionaries, is in the people of the state." This may seem to be a rather benign statement of fact. He was correct that the "people of the state" had sovereignty, but Story carefully chose his words. If the states could be reduced to little more than a collection of people within a geographic boundary or an administrative subdivision of the general government—as the Supreme Court had done in *McCulloch v. Maryland*, *Fletcher v. Peck*, *Martin v. Hunter's Lessee*, and *Cohens v. Virginia*—then every claim to state sovereignty was built on a foundation made of shifting sand instead of bedrock.[5]

Story then advanced that, "The colonies did not severally act for themselves, and proclaim their own independence." He acknowledged that some states had formed governments *before* the Declaration of Independence was approved, but he claimed this was only done because of the "recommendations of congress." Simply put, Story argued that the act of independence was advanced by the *people* of America in the aggregate and not the states. "It was," he declared, "the achievement of the whole for the benefit of the whole," and as such, as soon as the Continental Congress met in 1774, it began acting as the "national" legislature for the United States, meaning the United States was a "nation" and not a collection of states. "From the moment of the declaration of independence, if not for most purposes at an antecedent period...."[6]

This shrewd review of the American War for Independence and the Declaration missed the entire last paragraph of the document, and obviously so, for it refutes everything Story had contended to this point in his *Commentaries*. The United States was described as "them" and "they," meaning it was a plural collection of states united in common cause against the British crown, not a singular "United State" of consolidated "people." Jefferson purposely chose the term "state," and compared the "free and independent states" to the "state of Great Britain," itself a sovereign state. Jefferson also declared that each state could do "all acts and things" which "independent states may of right do," including war, peace, and commerce. That expressly recognizes state sovereignty. And Story neglected to tell the reader that several states issued separate declarations of independence and Great Britain recognized each state individually in the 1783 Treaty of Paris. It was not a treaty with the "United States" but with each of the thirteen states of North America. Story had several nationalist Supreme Court decisions on his side, namely from John Jay and Samuel Chase (Chase was impeached in 1804 for allowing his political leanings to influence cases), but not history.

Story shifted his discussion to the Articles of Confederation, where he deftly omitted any discussion of state sovereignty within the context of his previous attack on the existence of "free and independent" states. He dedicated most of the text to denouncing the defects of the Articles by attributing them to the loose confederation of independent states while failing to recognize that such a loose confederation was only possible if the Union was one of "states" and not "people." This was not a union "of the whole for the benefit of the whole" people. It was, as everyone at the time recognized, a union of "free and independent" states where state sovereignty was "expressly" protected in Article II of the Articles of

Confederation. Such language would not have been possible had the Union predated the states as Story contended just fifty pages earlier. Such inconsistency was commonplace, for after seemingly undermining his own version of American history, Story, in his discussion of the origins and nature of the Constitution, drifted right back to his argument that the people in the aggregate formed the Union.

Story dedicated considerable space in the *Commentaries* to refuting the work of Virginian St. George Tucker and his *View of the Constitution of the United States*. Though largely forgotten today, Tucker was a giant among early American legal scholars. His edited editions of William Blackstone's *Commentaries on the Laws of England* served as the primary legal text for American law students in the early nineteenth century. Even the Marshall court cited his edition of Blackstone in several leading decisions. Tucker organized the legal foundation for the "compact theory" of the Constitution, a "theory," more accurately termed a *fact*. His family dominated Virginia's legal education for decades and played an important role in the halls of Congress for much of antebellum American history. Tucker himself never served in Congress, but was twice appointed to the federal court system by Presidents James Madison and James Monroe, and he served for almost eight years on the Virginia Court of Appeals with Spencer Roane.

Tucker was a republican's republican who believed in the primacy of the law and the spirit of the Constitution as ratified by the state conventions. He did not sing hosannas to Madison and Hamilton's *Federalist* essays; instead, he understood the Constitution in light of the 1787 and 1788 written and spoken words of the "friends" of the document, the same men who Madison claimed gave the Constitution "all the authority which it possesses."[7] That Constitution was certainly at odds with that of the Marshall court. Tucker concluded that, "The constitution of the United States of America...is an original, written, federal, and social compact, freely, voluntarily, and solemnly entered into by the several states of North-America, and ratified by the people thereof, respectively...."[8]

But Story did not agree with Tucker's construction of the Constitution. He recoiled at the obvious implications of Tucker's views on the document, believing that the principles of the Virginia and Kentucky Resolutions of 1798 "flow[ed] naturally from the doctrines.... They go to the extent of reducing the government to a mere confederacy during pleasure; and of thus presenting the extraordinary spectacle of a nation existing only at the will of each of its constituent parts."[9] Story was in the midst of the "Nullification Crisis of 1832" when he penned these words. He wanted to reduce states' rights to a footnote in the annals of American history, a theory whose origins were little more than a historical lie crafted by devious political philosophers intent on destroying the Union of the founders.

Story had to labor to prove Tucker wrong. The definition of "compact" was racked and tortured to demonstrate that the Union was, after all, an agreement between the people in the aggregate. Story argued that, "There is nowhere found upon the face of the constitution any clause, intimating it to be a compact, or in anywise providing for its interpretation, as such..." and then used the Preamble to the Constitution to drive home his point.[10] This was a shrewd misrepresentation of the facts. Article VII of the Constitution—written in language that any lawyer (or judge) can understand—states that the Constitution is an agreement "between the States so ratifying the same." That would seem to indicate that the document was and is a compact between states, not the American people as a whole. Original drafts of the Preamble used the language "We the People of the States of..." followed by a list of every state rather than the ambiguous and truncated "We the People of the United States" in the final draft. This was done because Rhode Island did not send delegates to the Philadelphia Convention of 1787, and no one knew which states would ratify and which would not. Listing each state presumed complete agreement on the proposed Constitution. That could not be guaranteed by anyone in Philadelphia, particularly since Rhode Island dragged its feet on altering the general government. It would not ratify the Constitution until 1790, nearly two years after the document became official.

Story's plodding defense of national supremacy even used *anti-federalist* arguments to prove that the Constitution established a union of people not states. This turned the entire ratification process upside down. True, opponents of the document vocally attempted to make this point, but they were consistently shouted down by the friends of the document in every state ratifying convention and in the public presses. The common set of ideas found in the arguments from each convention and of each broadside in support of the document were that the Constitution maintained the Union as under the Articles of Confederation, the Senate—as agents of the states—served as the "federal" check on every branch of government, and the Preamble was nothing more than an introductory clause that affirmed that the "people of the states," not the people as a whole, ordained and established a "Constitution for the United States of America." Patrick Henry was famously promised this when he questioned why not "We the States" in the Virginia Ratifying Convention.[11] To say that the anti-federalists were right would be to willfully dismiss the volumes of ink and hours and hours of speeches made in defense of the Constitution. If Story's *Commentaries* are to be believed, then the ratification of the Constitution was the greatest con job in the history of the United States. That Hamilton lied is clear, but there were honest proponents of the document who firmly believed that federal power under the Constitution was limited by the language of the document itself and could not be enlarged through misconstruction.

Story left little doubt that his effort to refute the compact theory of the Constitution was aimed at establishing national supremacy and destroying the "Virginia school" of constitutional interpretation. He redundantly cited the supremacy clause of Article VI throughout his work in an effort to conclusively prove that the language of the Constitution supported his position and not that of Virginia. Story had waged war against their version of the Constitution in *Martin v. Hunter's Lessee* and in *Cohens v. Virginia*, but his *Commentaries* gave him a wider audience and a larger platform to push his constitutional ruminations. He concluded that, "We are to treat it, as it purports on its face to be, as a CONSTITUTION of government; and we are to reject all other appellations, and definitions of it, such, as that it is a compact, especially as they may mislead us into false constructions and glosses, and can have no tendency to instruct us in its real objects."[12] This was powerful ammunition for nationalists.

If, as Story suggested, the compact theory was little more than a "false construction," then implied powers must certainly be the intended mode of interpretation. Hamilton would have agreed, but that does not make either man correct. Story magically found the means for defending implied powers in the Preamble and in the decisions of the Marshall court, including *Martin v. Hunter's Lessee*, a decision he authored. "No interpretation of the words [in the Preamble]," he wrote, "in which those powers are granted, can be a sound one, which narrows down their ordinary import, so as to defeat those objects. That would be to destroy the spirit, and to cramp the letter." That phrase closely mirrored what both Marshall and Story himself delivered in separate cases. He then shockingly determined that Americans must "throw aside all notions of subjecting it [the Constitution] to a strict interpretation, as if it were subversive of the great interests of society, or derogated from the inherent sovereignty of the people." He later claimed, "There is no solid objection to implied powers."[13] Story was not interested in an evenhanded assessment of strict construction. The men who advanced this method of interpretation were some of the best legal minds in America, including the Father of the Constitution, Madison himself. Story was writing a thinly veiled polemic intended to discredit and embarrass his opponents.

Story also pulled off several marvelous examples of disingenuous wordsmithing by consistently using either the *Federalist* essays or the debates of the several state ratifying conventions out of context. For example, he attempted to argue that *Federalist* No. 32 proved that the Constitution intended to both subjugate the state governments and codify implied powers. That is a novel point. Hamilton insisted in *Federalist* No. 32 that the states retained their sovereignty in all cases but three: where the Constitution granted "express powers" to the general government; where Article 1, Section 10 prohibited the states from executing certain powers; "and where it granted an authority to the Union, to which a similar authority in the states would be absolutely and totally *contradictory* and *repugnant*." Story hung his hat on the last phrase. He thought this meant that Hamilton was arguing *for* the existence of implied powers, but Hamilton used the term "express powers" as a way to emphasize that powers were "expressly delegated" or granted to the central authority and that only those powers could be exercised by the general government. Hamilton did not outline what would constitute "totally *contradictory* and *repugnant*" authority but, placed within the context of the series, he was insisting that those powers were "express powers." That is not how Story interpreted the essay, but seemingly every "friend of the Constitution" understood it that way in 1788.[14] Hamilton, of course, was lying, but that weakens, not strengthens, Story's evidence.

Story made clear his intent in defending implied powers when he argued that, "if there be a conflict between the laws of the Union and the laws of the states, the former being supreme, the latter must of course yield. The possibility, nay the probability, of such a conflict was foreseen by the framers of the constitution, and was accordingly expressly provided for. If a state passes a law inconsistent with the constitution of the United States it is a mere nullity. If it passes a law clearly within its own constitutional powers, still if it conflicts with the exercise of a power given to congress, to the extent of the interference its operation is suspended; for, in a conflict of laws, that which is supreme must govern."[15] This is not how the supremacy clause was sold to the states during ratification. The qualifying phrase "in pursuance thereof" ensured that only *constitutional* laws and treaties were supreme. If the general government passed a law inconsistent with the "express powers" of the document, it would not be supreme and therefore void. In a conflict, then, between the state and the general government over such a law, the general government and not the state would be forced to yield. Story was conveniently cherry picking as he went along in order to defend the actions of the Marshall court for the preceding thirty years.

Story provided his most lasting and dangerous contribution to American constitutionalism when he wrote, "Words, from the necessary imperfection of all human language, acquire different shades of meaning, each of which is equally appropriate, and equally legitimate; each of which recedes in a wider or narrower degree from the others, according to circumstances; and each of which receives from its general use some indefiniteness and obscurity, as to its exact boundary and extent."[16] Put another way, Story suggested that the Constitution was open to vast interpretation that could not be confined by the language or the intent of the ratifiers. It was, to use a more modern phrase, a "living, breathing" document open to the "circumstances" of the time. In a phrase that mirrored John Marshall's opinion in *McCulloch v. Maryland*, Story declared that when interpreting the Constitution, "We may well resort to the meaning of single words to assist our inquiries, we should never forget, that it is an instrument of government we are to construe; and, as has been already stated, that must be the truest exposition, which best harmonizes with its design, its objects, and its general structure."[17] Story's *Commentaries* solidified the Marshall court's role in expounding the Constitution and gave rise to both the textual and implied interpretations of the document. He was by no means an originalist, even though he attempted to support his position by highlighting statements of various members of both the Philadelphia Convention and state ratification conventions.

As Story plodded through the various sections of the Constitution, he never abandoned his overall effort to reduce the "compact fact" of the Constitution to a "compact theory." For example, in his discussion of the Preamble, Story correctly contended that the introductory clause could not be used as a source of misconstruction. "It can never be the legitimate source of any implied power, when otherwise withdrawn from the constitution. Its true office is to expound the nature, and extent, and application of the powers actually conferred by the constitution, and not substantively to create them."[18] That sounds right. Madison often criticized those who placed too much emphasis on the Preamble as agents of "constructive ingenuity." But then Story reverted to his previous nationalist posture by maintaining:

> It is an ordinance or establishment of government and not a
> compact, though originating in consent; and it binds as a

fundamental law promulgated by the sovereign authority, and not as a compact or treaty entered into and *in fieri*, between each and all the citizens of the United States, as distinct parties. The language is, "We, the *people* of the United States," not, We, the *states*, "do *ordain* and *establish*;" not, do *contract* and enter into a *treaty* with each other; "this *constitution* for the United States of America," not this *treaty* between the several states. And it is, therefore, an unwarrantable assumption, not to call it a most extravagant stretch of interpretation, wholly at variance with the language, to substitute other words and other senses for the words and senses incorporated, in this solemn manner, into the substance of the instrument itself. We have the strongest assurances, that this preamble was not adopted as a mere formulary; but as a solemn promulgation of a fundamental fact, vital to the character and operations of the government. The obvious object was to substitute a government of the people, for a confederacy of states; a constitution for a compact.[19]

This tortured logic seems to fit with Story's insistence on ridding the Preamble of misconstruction, only to Story, "misconstruction" means how every proponent of the Constitution sold the document to the states during ratification. That is not misconstruction. Story usefully forgot every state check on the federal system, from the Electoral College, to the Senate, to the fact that should a tie occur in the election of a president, voting in the House of Representatives would be by state and not by individual members. That had already happened twice when Story published his *Commentaries*. That would seem to indicate that the Constitution was a compact or contract between the ratifying parties. Story ultimately failed to answer the single most pressing question for the nationalists: if the Constitution established "a more perfect Union," what Union were the framers and ratifiers discussing? Was it the Union that existed before the Constitution as under the Articles of Confederation, in that case a union of states, or was it an entirely new creation? Answering that question would invalidate their core beliefs, for though Story wrote that the Constitution sought "to substitute a government of the people for a confederacy of states; a constitution for a compact," neither the language of the document nor the public intent of the ratifers supports that position.

Predictably, Story's discussion of congressional powers confirmed the loose construction position. He defended an expansive interpretation of the necessary and proper clause by denying that strict constructionists like St. George Tucker had any legal leg to stand on. This was classic Hamiltonian deception, even to the point of citing Hamilton's defense of the First Bank of the United States to prove his point. You can't prove a lie with a lie, but Story tried. Story argued Congress had the constitutional ability to incorporate a bank, fund internal improvements, and in short do every act that strict constructionists insisted for decades was incompatible with an original interpretation of the document.

He dedicated a substantial section of Volume III to the Supreme Court. Story did not miss the opportunity to cement John Marshall's vision for a powerful (and supreme) federal judiciary. He dusted off the decisions of *Martin v. Hunter's Lessee* and *Cohens v. Virginia* to defend federal judicial supremacy by claiming that, "Even if there were no danger of collision between the laws and powers of the Union, and those of the states, it is utterly impossible, that, without some superintending judiciary establishment, there could be any uniform administration, or interpretation of them. The idea of uniformity of decision by thirteen independent and co-ordinate tribunals (and the number is now advanced to twenty-four) is absolutely visionary, if not absurd. The consequence would necessarily be, that neither the constitution, nor the laws, neither the rights and powers of the Union, nor those of the states, would be the same in any two states."[20] This was a direct attack on the Richmond Junto, who for years had claimed that state courts would be adequate to enforce *constitutional* federal legislation. To Story and Marshall, this was dangerous and imbecilic.

Story did not leave any expansive reading of the Constitution by the Marshall court undefended. He found judicial review consistent with original intent, heaped praise on the Marshall court's handling of landmark cases, asserted the importance of the federal court system to the stability of the Union, and considered the Supreme Court to be the true defender of American liberty. That's quite a list for an institution that faced constant scrutiny for nearly all of its existence. Story chalked up this opposition to strict constructionist distortion of original intent. Story primarily focused his attention on St. George Tucker's *Views of the Constitution*, but the Richmond Junto, John Taylor of Caroline, John C. Calhoun, and every proponent of strict construction were indirectly attacked through their close association with Tucker's constitutional interpretation. Story's *Commentaries*, then, was little more than a verbose diatribe clothed with the legal authority and the trappings of the Supreme Court.

Lavish praise for Story's *Commentaries* among both contemporary and modern readers has led to an unfortunate ignorance of opposition to his interpretations. A black hole is a more appropriate description. Very few, if any, modern law students will read Tucker's *Views of the Constitution*, though it was *the* standard commentary on the Constitution until 1833, and still fewer (if that's possible) will have been exposed to John Taylor of Caroline's *New Views on the Constitution of the United States* published in 1823 or Abel P. Upshur's 1840 publication of *A Brief Enquiry into the True Nature and Character of Our Federal Government*. Story was certainly aware of Taylor's commentary. The historian R. Kent Newmyer suggests that Taylor's work drove Story "into a Burkean rage."[21] This might be an exaggeration, for Story personally liked Taylor, but there was little doubt that Story intended his *Commentaries* to not only replace Tucker's version of Blackstone but to destroy Taylor's assessment of the Union and the Constitution.

Taylor's *New Views of the Constitution* was the opposite of Story's *Commentaries* in every way. Whereas Story considered the United States to be a "national sovereignty" given authority by a singular people, Taylor emphasized that a federal union could only be formed by sovereign political states, not an amorphous mass of people. Taylor anticipated Story's arguments when he wrote in 1823 that the word federal, "implies a league between sovereign nations, has been so used by all classes of people from the commencement of our political existence down to this day, and is inapplicable to a nation consolidated under one sovereignty."[22] The United States general government, then, being formed under a federal model, could never be considered a consolidated nation. Of course, the component parts of this federal model were "states," a conscious word choice in 1776. Taylor argued that because the union was formed between states, there could be little doubt that the states had complete sovereign authority in the government. "As no word more explicitly comprises the idea of a sovereign independent community; as it is used in conjunction with a declared sovereignty and independence; as it is retained by the union of 1787, and in all the operations of our governments; and as sovereign powers only could be reserved by states; there seems to be no sound argument by which it can be deprived of its intrinsick [sic] meaning, contrary to these positive constructions."[23] Story's commentaries could be listed among "these positive constructions."

Taylor further lanced Story's "one people" boil with skillful precision. Calling this position "the crime of selfmurder," Taylor labeled the "one people" theorists skillful "metaphysicians" who aimed "to puzzle mankind in their search after truth...." Taylor considered the only remedy to be "the resistance of common sense, and the dictates of unsophisticated conscience." He argued that the "one people" argument was newly crafted by these "metaphysicians" and had no basis in history. "But the achievement of losing twenty-four sovereign states by the acuteness of construction, and getting rid of a people in each, by means of the word necessary to describe them, was reserved for the refined politicians of the present day; and is equivalent to the ingenuity of a fisherman, who should lose a whale by a definition of his name, which would destroy his qualities."[24] If this analogy wasn't potent enough, Taylor concisely destroyed the one people thesis later in the book. "There are many states in America, but no state of America, nor any people of an American state. A constitution for America or Americans, would therefore have been similar to a constitution for Utopia or Utopians."[25]

Taylor's *New Views* was based on both the journals of the Philadelphia Convention and the *Federalist* essays. He did not have access to the notes of the separate state ratifying conventions, but his thorough examination of the available material in 1823 made him the first originalist. Story utilized the same sources for his *Commentaries*, but Story relied more on the decisions of the Supreme Court to defend his conclusions than the documents produced during the debates over the creation and ratification of the Constitution. Story's reliance on the "common law" of the United States federal judiciary set him apart from Taylor and put Story at odds with the American tradition of written constitutions. Taylor rightly contends that, "Had the journal of the convention which framed the constitution of the United States, though obscure and incomplete, been published immediately after its ratification, it would have furnished lights towards a true construction, sufficiently clear to have prevented several trespasses upon its principles, and tendencies towards its subversion."[26] Story may have agreed with this sentiment in part, but he would have considered both Taylor and Tucker to be the subversives. But history was not on his side, as Taylor artfully proved.

Abel Upshur had the ability to review Story's *Commentaries* before he published his *Brief Enquiry* in 1840. It was subsequently republished in the 1860s in the *North* as a constitutional defense of the right of secession. That alone made the book scandalous and regulated it to the perpetual blacklist of subversive American treatises. It should not be so poorly regarded. Upshur was a distinguished statesman from the Eastern Shore of Virginia. He was not considered part of the Richmond Junto but he shared their principles and became an active conservative in Virginia state politics. He served as a delegate to the Virginia Constitutional Convention of 1829–30 and supported South Carolina's efforts to nullify the federal tariff in 1832. He penned a series of essays in defense of the Virginia and Kentucky Resolutions of 1798 for *The Examiner, and Journal of Political Economy*, a biweekly publication dedicated to states' rights edited by Philadelphia economist Condy Raguet. He was later appointed secretary of the Navy by President John Tyler and then secretary of state where in

1844, after just seven months in office, he was tragically killed in a freak accident on the USS *Princeton*.

Upshur shared both Taylor's and Tucker's views on the Constitution, but his work condensed the positions of both men into a concise and readable explanation of the originalist position. He first sought to debunk the myth that a singular American people wrote and ratified the Constitution. This was the heart of Story's *Commentaries* and every nationalist argument from the late eighteenth century forward. Upshur wrote that Story's "desire to make 'the people of the United States' into one consolidated nation is so strong and predominant, that it breaks forth, often uncalled for, in every part of his work."[27] Upshur then proceeded to prove Story wrong. "The *unity* contended for by the author no where appears, but is distinctly disaffirmed in every sentence...."[28] Whereas Story's nationalist lens saw unity among the colonists, a new "nation" so to speak, Upshur proved that Story's nationalism was an imaginative construction fabricated out of thin air. "The people of the American colonies were, in no conceivable sense, 'one people'.... The colonies had no common legislature, no common treasury, no common military power, no common judicatory.... Although they were all, alike, dependencies of the British Crown, yet, even in the action of the parent country...they were recognized as separate and distinct."[29]

This was only the beginning. Upshur shredded every portion of Story's arguments. Story believed the Continental Congress served as a *de facto* "national government" for the United States. Wrong. Upshur wrote, "Congress did not claim any legislative power whatever.... Its acts were in the form of *resolutions* and not in the form of *laws*; It *recommended* to its constituents whatever it believed to be for their advantage, but it *commanded* nothing"[emphasis mine].[30] He attacked Story's version of the Preamble and the relationship between the states and the general authority. "The Constitution," he thundered, "is federative in the power which framed it; federative in the power which adopted and ratified it; federative in the power which sustains and keeps it alive; federative in the power by which alone it can be altered or amended; and federative in the structure of all its departments." If that was the case,

Upshur rhetorically asks, "In what respect...can it be justly called a consolidated or national government?"[31]

Having trampled the "one people" and "nationalist" interpretation of the document, Upshur pivoted to the most pressing issue in Story's *Commentaries*, that of "the final judge or interpreter in constitutional controversies." Story, of course, sided with the federal judiciary. Upshur understood why the nationalists were "dazzled" by the thought of unlimited federal power. The prospect would be enticing for any political agenda, but particularly for one that required the support of the general government, namely a national economic program consisting of central banking, high tariffs, and federally-funded internal improvements. By 1840, that program had been repackaged under the slick marketing term the "American System." Gone was the stigma attached to Hamilton, but it was still his baby and it was that type of political-economic system Story defended. Upshur reasonably asked what, if Story is correct, would be the limits on federal authority? "Shall the agent be permitted to judge of the extent of his own powers, without reference to his constituent?"[32]

Upshur reasonably—though scandalously today—concluded that state action against the general government was the only way to "prevent the Constitution from being violated...." Real federalism as outlined by the Tenth Amendment and articulated by the Virginia and Kentucky Resolutions of 1798 presented the only possible check on the powers of the general government. He had no faith that any branch of the general government would willingly surrender its own power, particularly if usurped from another branch in the system, including the states. That had been made clear in the first sixty years of American government under the Constitution. Upshur cogently argued that "nullification" or "state interposition" was built into the system itself. "As that Constitution was formed by sovereign States, they alone are authorized, whenever the question arises between them and their common government, to determine, in the last resort, what powers they intended to confer on it. This is an inseparable incident of sovereignty; a right which belongs to the States, simply because they have never surrendered it to any other power." Upshur then warned of the consequences of surrendering this power to a national authority like the Supreme Court. "If their people suffer them to sink into the insignificance of mere municipal corporations, it will be vain to invoke their protection against the gigantic power of the federal government. This is the point to which the vigilance of the people should be chiefly directed. Their highest interest is at home; their palladium is their own State governments.... It is vain to hope that the federative principle of our government can be preserved, or that any thing can prevent it from running into the absolutism of consolidation, if we suffer the rights of the States to be filched away, and their dignity and influence to be lost, through our carelessness or neglect."[33]

This may seem like the unsubstantiated though enlightened ramblings of a Virginia partisan. Upshur was certainly more philosophical than Story but no less prescient. This became clear when he predicted the inevitable outcome of Story's nationalist interpretation of the Constitution. "If [Story's] principles be correct, if ours be, indeed, a consolidated and not a federative system, I, at least, have no praises to bestow on it. Monarchy in form, open and acknowledged, is infinitely preferable to monarchy in disguise." Nevertheless, Story's Constitution would produce monarchy. This is perhaps where Upshur was the most perceptive. Hamilton's nationalist meddling in Washington's second term led to an unconstitutional expansion of executive power, and Upshur lived through Andrew Jackson's full throttle stampede of a presidency. He wasn't called "King Andrew" for nothing.

To Upshur, the natural result of centralization would be—and had been—the ascendency of the American presidency to the status of an elected king. "In every age of the world," he lamented, "the few have found means to steal power from the many. But in *our* government, if it be indeed a consolidated one, such a result is absolutely inevitable. The powers which are expressly lodged in the executive, and the still greater powers which are assumed, because the Constitution does not expressly deny them, a patronage which has no limit, and acknowledges no responsibility, all these are quite enough to bring the legislature to the feet of the executive. Every new power, therefore, which is assumed by the *federal government*, does but add so much to the powers of the president.

One by one, the powers of the other departments are swept away, or are wielded only at the will of the executive." Upshur insisted that the net result of this would be to "raise the president above the people." That had never been the objective of true American liberty and government or the original intent of the Constitution. The president "is not, by the Constitution, and never was designed to be, any thing more than a simple executive of the laws; but the principle which consolidates all power in the federal government clothes him with royal authority, and subjects every right and every interest of the people to his will."[34] That was Hamilton's plan all along.

Joseph Story's *Commentaries* has served as the nationalist playbook for Constitutional interpretation for nearly 180 years. Hamilton could not have written it better. At the same time, the works of Tucker, Taylor, and Upshur have been largely lost to American legal scholars, in part because all three men were slaveholders (Tucker was an early abolitionist), but also because they advanced an interpretation of the Constitution at odds with the dominant Hamiltonian myth of absolute federal supremacy with expansive implied powers. Hamilton's political economic system backed by loose construction eventually wound up in Marshall's court where it was largely upheld, but without Story's *Commentaries* training future generations of American lawyers, even conservatives, Hamilton's America may have met insurmountable legal obstacles. The fact that Story has morphed into a popular conservative legal hero today proves that the definition of originalism has been distorted and co-opted by the Hamiltonian nationalists. If Story was an originalist then so was Hamilton, and no one should make that claim.

CHAPTER 12

HUGO BLACK AND INCORPORATION

Hamilton's constitutional revolution remained incomplete until the 1960s. Loose construction generally dominated American political thought, and nationalism was the accepted version of the American founding after the conclusion of the War Between the States in 1865, but the Bill of Rights, specifically the Tenth Amendment, remained a stumbling block in the rush to reduce the states to mere corporations of the general government. That had been Hamiltonian dream since 1787. State powers and the truly federal features of the Constitution, namely state equality in the Senate and the Electoral College, prevented a wholesale takeover of the general government by the nationalists, but by the 1870s there were warning signs that Washington, DC would eventually swallow up the states and render them incapable of stopping the march of centralization. Certainly the war helped. States' rights became a pejorative term in the postbellum period, and the Supreme Court became the cleanup hitter in the final push toward Hamilton's America. "Incorporation" of the Bill of Rights against the states through the Fourteenth Amendment was the last step in the nationalist triumph.[1]

It didn't start off that way. In fact, the majority of the founding generation rejected the application of the Bill of Rights against the states. James Madison first presented the idea in June 1789. His proposed fifth amendment would have added the language, "No state shall violate the equal rights of conscience, or the freedom of the press, or the trial by jury in criminal cases" to Article I, Section 10 of the Constitution.[2] He considered this proposed amendment "the most valuable...in the whole list. If there was any reason to restrain the Government of the United States from infringing upon these essential rights, it was equally necessary that they should be secured against the State Governments." Only Thomas Tudor Tucker of South Carolina opposed it initially. He argued that the Congress should leave the states alone and "not...interfere with them more than we already do."[3] Madison's proposed incorporation amendment, however, never made it past the final cut, and the preamble to the Bill of Rights expressly stated that the ten ratified amendments were "restrictive clauses" intended to "prevent misconstruction or abuse of its powers." The Bill of Rights applied only to the general government, not the states, even if Madison thought it would be wise to place restrictions on state legislatures in regard to three civil liberties. Tucker's view, not Madison's, became the standard interpretation of the Bill of Rights.

John Marshall had the opportunity to enforce Madison's incorporation dream in 1833, but in a moment of clarity he refused to enlarge the powers of the general government at the expense of the states. This was one of only a handful of times when Marshall could have been classified as an originalist. The case of *Barron v. Baltimore* set the tone for the division between the states and the general government in relation to civil liberties for over one hundred years. The plaintiffs in the case, John Barron and John Craig, sued the mayor and city council of Baltimore for damages after the city diverted several streams away from their wharf business in Baltimore harbor to improve and construct new streets in the city. This resulted in shallows around the wharf, making it too dangerous to conduct business. Barron and Craig claimed this violated the Fifth

Amendment's prohibition on uncompensated eminent domain. Because the Bill of Rights prohibited the general government from using private property without just compensation, the city of Baltimore could not legally seize private property without paying for it. This was the first time anyone had proposed enforcing the Bill of Rights against the states in the federal court system.

Marshall's unanimous majority opinion was concurrently terse and far-reaching. He insisted that, "The people of the United States framed such a government for the United States as they supposed best adapted to their situation, and best calculated to promote their interests. The powers they conferred on this government were to be exercised by itself; and the limitations on power, if expressed in general terms, are naturally, and, we think, necessarily applicable to the government created by the instrument. They are limitations of power granted in the instrument itself; not of distinct governments, framed by different persons and for different purposes." Plainly put, Marshall concluded that, "In almost every convention by which the constitution was adopted, amendments to guard against the abuse of power were recommended. These amendments demanded security against the apprehended encroachments of the general government—not against those of the local governments. In compliance with a sentiment thus generally expressed, to quiet fears thus extensively entertained, amendments were proposed by the required majority in Congress, and adopted by the states. These amendments contain no expression indicating an intention to apply them to the state governments. This court cannot so apply them."[4] While Marshall's understanding of who framed and ratified the Constitution is debatable, his conclusion that the restrictions placed within the document both in the text itself and through the Bill of Rights applied only to the general government and not to the states is buttressed by history.

Enter Justice Hugo Black, one of the most transformational legal figures in American history. Born in Harlan, Alabama in 1886, Black was a self-described "clay county hillbilly."[5] He and Marshall shared a common upbringing. Both were rough-hewn frontiersman. Black was reared on a 320-acre farm in the hills of north Alabama. Not much had changed in material life for rural Southerners since the early nineteenth century. They lived in the dirt and worked the land. Life was hard and economic opportunity, particularly in the postbellum South, was sparse. Black's father, William Lafayette Black, eventually saved enough money to move to Ashville, Alabama. He bought a general store and enrolled his children in school. In time, W. L. Black became a prosperous merchant, and Hugo Black benefitted from his father's determined efforts to rid his family of poverty. Hugo Black, however, never forsook his homespun roots. Like Marshall who often donned his coonskin cap, Black took pride in his rugged upbringing.

Black graduated with a law degree from the University of Alabama in 1906, and after his fledgling law office burned down in Ashland, he moved to Birmingham, a "New South" city with a booming industrial economy and a Puritanical backbone. While the ironworkers drowned their sorrows and sought escape from the "gates of hell" in bars and brothels, city leaders passed "blue laws" that outlawed most amusements on Sundays. This was an extension of the progressivism that swept the United States in the late nineteenth century. Jim Crow segregation, sin laws, and industrial muscle highlighted Birmingham's claim of being a modern Southern city. Black supported every element of this progressive agenda. As solicitor for Jefferson County from 1915–17, Black vigorously enforced the newly enacted state prohibition laws. He also defended a Methodist minister charged with killing a Catholic priest after the priest married the Methodist minister's daughter to an alleged black man (he was from Puerto Rico but did not look black).

Black eventually joined the Ku Klux Klan. This was a logical decision for a progressive in the 1920s. The Jazz Age Klan had full-throated support from many white leaders in American society, North and South. Its nationalist agenda aimed at ridding American—not just Southern—society of immigrants, blacks, and Jews. Progressives such as Margaret Sanger made it a point to lecture to Klan groups. They shared a similar vision. Black believed in the Klan's moral code and anti-Catholic agenda, so much so that this guided his judicial opinions on the Supreme Court.

Though he had long substituted white robes for black, Justice Black never relinquished his anti-Catholic bigotry.

Black's involvement in the Klan helped in his bid for the United States Senate in 1926. Incumbent Senator Oscar Underwood retired that year, largely due to his longstanding opposition to the Klan. He was threatened and informed that he had lost support from the state's Democratic Party. Black seemed to be a logical choice for the job. He won in a landslide and became a leading figure in the Democratic Party. He enthusiastically backed Franklin Roosevelt's New Deal and campaigned for Roosevelt in both 1932 and 1936. As payback, Roosevelt nominated Black for the Supreme Court in 1937. The Senate confirmed his appointment 63-16. This may have been Roosevelt's most important selection for the federal bench, largely because Black changed the way the American legal system viewed both the Bill of Rights and the first section of the Fourteenth Amendment. He was the driving force behind incorporation of the Bill of Rights against the states in the twentieth century. Any time an American claims a "constitutional right" to same-sex marriage or abortion, Hugo Black is behind it.

Until Justice Black took the bench, no federal judge had disputed Marshall's interpretation of federalism and the Bill of Rights in *Barron v. Baltimore*. The court had, in fact, explicitly upheld Marshall's position. In 1873, several white butchers in New Orleans sued Louisiana in federal court under the claim that their constitutional rights as protected by the first section of the Fourteenth Amendment had been violated. What this really meant was that they believed their "civil liberties" had been trampled by Louisiana law. This was the first time the court had been given the opportunity to adjudicate on the Fourteenth Amendment, and at stake was the entire understanding of federalism. Did the Fourteenth Amendment's protection of "life, liberty, and property" apply to state legislation, or did Marshall's view of federalism in *Barron v. Baltimore* still reign supreme?

Justice Samuel Miller delivered the majority opinion for a divided court. An Abraham Lincoln appointee, Miller had been a staunch abolitionist before the Civil War and supported much of Lincoln's political agenda in the 1860s, including his broad use of executive powers during the war and the suppression of states' rights. He also favored equal treatment for former slaves under the law. He was certainly a progressive for his time and, like Marshall, a nationalist judge. Republicans and even many Democrats thought so highly of his legal philosophy and impeccable credentials that they confirmed his appointment in thirty minutes.[6] As such, his opinion in the Slaughterhouse Cases should be instructive for interpreting the Fourteenth Amendment.

The first section of the Fourteenth Amendment reads, "All persons born or naturalized in the United States, and subject to the jurisdiction thereof, are citizens of the United States and of the state wherein they reside. No state shall make or enforce any law which shall abridge the privileges or immunities of citizens of the United States; nor shall any state deprive any person of life, liberty, or property, without due process of law; nor deny to any person within its jurisdiction the equal protection of the laws." The New Orleans butchers suggested that Louisiana denied or deprived them of the "privileges and immunities," their "equal protection under the law," and their "property without due process of the law."

Miller thought otherwise. If the court ruled in favor of the butchers, Congress would be given the authority to "pass laws in advance, limiting and restricting the exercise of legislative power by the States, in their most ordinary and usual functions, as in its judgment it may think proper on all such subjects." Furthermore, Miller correctly reasoned that, "such a construction followed by the reversal of the judgments of the Supreme Court of Louisiana in these cases, would constitute this court a perpetual censor upon all legislation of the States, on the civil rights of their own citizens, with authority to nullify such as it did not approve as consistent with those rights, as they existed at the time of the adoption of this amendment." Miller unmistakably foresaw the impact a misapplication of the Fourteenth Amendment would have on both the states and the Constitution itself. He wrote, "These consequences are so serious, so far-reaching and pervading, so great a departure from the structure and spirit of our institutions; when the effect is to fetter and degrade the State governments by subjecting them to the control of Congress, in the exercise of powers heretofore universally conceded to them of the most ordinary and fundamental character; when in fact it radically changes the whole theory of the relations of the State and Federal governments to each other and of both these governments to the people...." The only imaginable conclusion under these circumstances was to reject such an interpretation because "no such results were intended by the Congress which proposed these amendments, nor by the legislatures of the States which ratified them."

As a good nationalist, Miller believed "the true danger to the perpetuity of the Union was in the capacity of the State organizations to combine and concentrate all the powers of the State, and of contiguous States, for a determined resistance to the General Government..." But he could not find any evidence that the Fourteenth Amendment had "any purpose to destroy the main features of the general system..." including state powers of "regulation of civil rights—the rights of person and of property...." There was a sharp distinction, Miller contended, between state and federal citizenship. "Not only may a man be a citizen of the United States without being a citizen of a State, but...He must reside within the State to make him a citizen of it, but it is only necessary that he should be born or naturalized in the United States to be a citizen of the Union."[7] The court struck down this nationalist usurpation of power as a corruption of the original meaning and intent of the Fourteenth Amendment. But was Miller correct in his decision?

Congress began floating proposals for an amendment to the Constitution that would offer "equal protection" to "all persons...in their life, liberty, and property" as early as 1866.[8] Representative John Bingham of Ohio was the pioneer in this movement. Hugo Black called him the "Father of the Fourteenth Amendment," and Bingham represented the more radical wing of the Republican Party of the 1860s. He had been elected to Congress in the 1850s as a Republican but failed to win reelection in 1862 when Democrat Joseph White trounced him in the midterm election. This may have been because many Ohioans believed Bingham advocated black suffrage (a charge he publicly denied), an unpopular position in certain regions of the state. Regardless, this worked to his advantage. Abraham Lincoln tapped Bingham to serve as the judge advocate of the Union army shortly after his defeat. Bingham seized the opportunity and ultimately acted in this role in the trial against the Lincoln assassination conspirators. After again being elected to Congress in 1865, he was appointed lead counsel in the thinly veiled witch-hunt known as the 1868 impeachment trial of Andrew Johnson. Bingham was as partisan as anyone in Congress. His ardent anti-Southern views and intractable personality served the Republican Party well during both the War and Reconstruction, and very few members of Congress matched either his intensity or loyalty to the radical Republican agenda. That included the future Fourteenth Amendment.

The Republican-controlled Congress of the 1860s was rather creative in its constitutional philosophy. From supporting unconstitutional executive powers to passing legislation that had been considered constitutionally dubious for nearly eighty years, the rank-and-file Republicans of the 1860s recreated the Constitution as they went. This included "incorporation" of the Bill of Rights. For example, in 1866, Vermont-born Representative Robert Hale of New York said of the proposed Fourteenth Amendment, "Now, what are these amendments to the Constitution, numbered from one to ten, one of which is the fifth article in question?.... They constitute the bill of rights, a bill of rights for the protection of the citizen, and defining and limiting the power of Federal and State legislation."[9] Senator William Morris Stewart of Nevada argued that the Constitution formed "the vital, sovereign, and controlling part of the fundamental law of every State...." State bill of rights simply recognized "the politically omniscient and omnipresent sovereignty [of] the national fundamental law. No State can adopt anything in a State constitution in conflict."[10] This would have been news to every member of the founding generation, including John Marshall and Alexander Hamilton.

When Representative Michael Kerr of Indiana called out the Republicans for their ignorance of the *Barron v. Baltimore* decision, Martin Thayer of Pennsylvania retorted, "Of what value are those guarantees if you deny all power on the part of the Congress of the United States to execute and enforce them?"[11] This became the standard battle cry for the Republican Party during Reconstruction. Many former slaves were denied the ability to own or possess firearms, and Republicans often insisted that the leadership in the reconstructed Southern states recognize, i.e. incorporate, the Bill of Rights. When that failed to materialize, congressional Republicans, led by Bingham, worked to make that happen, though to what extent they pushed for full application of the Bill of Rights against the states or to what extent Congress accepted this position is debatable. The historical record, in fact, makes it clear that Bingham did not consider the Fourteenth Amendment to be a blanket guarantee of "incorporation."

Bingham proposed the Fourteenth Amendment as a way to guarantee that the provisions of the Civil Rights Act of 1866 would be upheld in federal court. The object of that legislation was to ensure that former slaves could own property, sue in federal court, and sit on juries, nothing more. Bingham, however, played fast and loose with both the language of the Constitution and the original intent of the Bill of Rights. He insisted that his amendment stood "in the very words of the Constitution...Every word...is today in the Constitution." This was only partly true. Bingham's amendment stated that the Fifth Amendment guaranteed "equal protection in the rights of life, liberty, and property," but the Fifth Amendment did not include the phrase "equal protection" at all. Bingham lamented that "These great provisions of the Constitution, this immortal bill of rights embodied in the Constitution, rested for its execution and enforcement hitherto upon the fidelity of the States."[12] His amendment would change that.

But what were "these great provisions of the Constitution?" Virtually every supporter of the amendment believed they were confined to the "privileges and immunities" clause of Article IV and the protection of due process in the Fifth Amendment. Only a couple of radical Republicans discussed freedom of speech, the press, or religion, for example, or the right to "keep and bear arms" unless firearms were considered property. Representative Frederick E. Woodbridge of Vermont argued that Bingham's amendment was "intended to enable Congress by its enactments when necessary to give a citizen of the United States in whatever State he may be, those privileges and immunities which are guaranteed to him under the Constitution of the United States...[and] the inalienable rights of life and liberty and...that protection to his property which is extended to other citizens of the State."[13]

Senator Jacob M. Howard of Michigan offered the only substantial voice that conflicted with the majority opinion. Howard was a radical Republican who was consistently outvoted on the joint committee tasked with drafting and explaining the amendment. When the committee chair William Fessenden of Maine became too ill to lead the committee, Howard took over and attempted to interpret the "the views and motives which influence the committee." To Howard, the Fourteenth Amendment was designed to protect the "privileges and immunities" outlined in the Constitution, and to that "should be added the personal rights guaranteed and secured by the first eight amendments."[14] No one immediately challenged Howard's statement, but earlier Senator Luke Poland of Vermont had contradicted Howard by insisting, "The clause...that 'no State shall...abridge the privileges and immunities of citizens of the United States' secures nothing beyond what was intended by the original provision in the Constitution."[15]

Woodbridge and Poland were making an important point that was later upheld by Justice Miller in the Slaughterhouse Cases. The "privileges and immunities clause" of the Constitution was directly lifted from the Articles of Confederation by the Framers at the 1787 Philadelphia Convention and carried no new meanings in the Constitution. When both Woodbridge and Poland contended that Bingham's amendment would guarantee "those privileges and immunities" of the Constitution, he was referring to Article IV, Section 1, while the protection of "life, liberty, and property" was specifically addressed by the Fifth Amendment. By making former slaves citizens of the United States, the Fourteenth Amendment authorized Congress at the very most to offer them Fifth Amendment protection. This was noted by Representative James F. Wilson of Iowa when he remarked that, "I find in the bill of rights which the gentleman desires to have enforced by an amendment...that

'No person shall be deprived of life, liberty, and property without due process of law.' I understand that these constitute the civil rights…to which this bill relates, having nothing to do with subjects committed to the control of the several States."[16] The majority of the Congress in 1866 thought that no other amendment other than potentially the Fifth Amendment in the Bill of Rights could be applied against the states by the Fourteenth Amendment.

Bingham himself demonstrated this, though his thinking on the issue was often muddled and historically inaccurate. In his opening speech presenting the Fourteenth Amendment, Bingham thought that the Bill of Rights was already applicable against the states through the supremacy clause found in Article VI of the Constitution. After opponents of his amendment shredded that argument, Bingham conceded that Marshall's opinion in *Barron v. Baltimore* did indeed acknowledge that the Bill of Rights did not apply to the states, and "that the citizens must rely upon the State for their protection. I admit that such is the rule under the Constitution as it stands." But that didn't matter. In Bingham's imaginative construction, "A State has not the right to deny equal protection…in the rights of life, liberty, and property." Why? Because "although as ruled the existing amendments…do not bind the States, they are nevertheless to be enforced and observed in the States."[17] It was not unusual for Republicans to dust off this type of Hamiltonian nationalism to support their positions. To the Republican Party, the war simply reinforced the long-held nationalist fantasy of reducing the states to mere corporate entities of the general government. What the framers of the Fourteenth Amendment did not accomplish, however, Hugo Black would.

In 1944, African American Dewey Adamson was arrested and charged with burglary and first degree murder in California. Knowing that his prior criminal record would be used against him in court, Adamson refused to testify in his own defense. The prosecutor used this against him, claiming that a refusal to testify implied guilt under a little-used California statute. Adamson was found guilty and sentenced to death. His defense attorney appealed the case to the California Supreme Court, arguing that Adamson's Fifth Amendment rights had been violated by the state of California. That court disagreed and upheld the decision of the lower court. Adamson's defense team then appealed to the United States Supreme Court in 1947.

This was a clear-cut case of incorporation. The only way Adamson could appeal on a Fifth Amendment basis was if the Fourteenth Amendment had incorporated the Fifth against California law. The Slaughterhouse Cases in 1873 had already rejected this interpretation, but Adamson's legal team had no other arrows left in their quiver. This was their last-ditch effort to save Adamson's life. The court took the case as *Adamson v. California* and quickly upheld the decision of the California Supreme Court. Writing for the majority, Justice Stanley Forman Reed argued that had this case been tried in a federal court, Adamson would have been protected by the Fifth Amendment, but because the Supreme Court had already decided on several occasions, beginning with *Barron v. Baltimore* in 1833, that the Bill of Rights did not apply to the states, the decision of the California Supreme Court would stand. The decision wasn't unanimous, however, and Justice Black used the opportunity to outline his views on incorporation. His dissent was one of the more important legal treatises of the twentieth century.

Black argued in his dissent that, "My study of the historical events that culminated in the Fourteenth Amendment, and the expressions of those who sponsored and favored, as well as those who opposed, its submission and passage persuades me that one of the chief objects that the provisions of the Amendment's first section, separately and as a whole, were intended to accomplish was to make the Bill of Rights, applicable to the states." To prove this, Black launched into a discussion of the drafting and ratification of the Fourteenth Amendment that relied heavily on the statements of both Senator Howard and Representative Bingham in 1866. He called Bingham "the Madison of the first section of the Fourteenth Amendment," and argued that the evidence unequivocally supported his belief that the framers of the Fourteenth Amendment intended the first eight amendments in the Bill of Rights to be incorporated against every state in the Union.[18] This was a lazy reading of the evidence. Black did not take into account the several statements made in the Congress against this interpretation of the Fourteenth Amendment, nor did he acknowledge that even Bingham himself waffled on the amendment's meaning and intent, but that didn't matter. Hugo Black became the leading proponent of the "Incorporation Doctrine." His dissent was the opening salvo in a decades-long assault on federalism and the meaning and intent of both the original Constitution and the Fourteenth Amendment.

Nineteen forty-seven marked a watershed in American legal history. Not only had Black picked up his pen and rewritten history in his *Adamson v. California* dissent, but he applied the same sloppy research and historical revisionism to his landmark majority opinion in *Everson v. Board of Education of the Township of Ewing*. The New Jersey legislature passed a law requiring that all children attending either public or private schools be given free busing. Arch R. Everson sued the state in federal court, arguing that the use of public funds in busing children to Catholic schools, as required by the law, violated the First Amendment to the Constitution and its legal pronouncement of "separation of church and state." How could that be? Through the Fourteenth Amendment's incorporation of the First Amendment, of course.

The Supreme Court had already pulled off a legal coup in this regard just seven years prior in the case of *Cantwell v. Connecticut* (1940). In that case, the unanimous court (including Black) held that the first section of the Fourteenth Amendment incorporated the First Amendment against the state of Connecticut, but made no explanation as to how it decided to reverse nearly 150 years of legal history. Justice Owen Roberts tersely stated for the majority that, "The fundamental concept of liberty embodied in [the Fourteenth] Amendment embraces the liberties guaranteed by the First Amendment. The First Amendment declares that Congress shall make no law respecting an establishment of religion or prohibiting the free exercise thereof. The Fourteenth Amendment has rendered the legislatures of the states as incompetent as Congress to enact such laws."[19] Black used the Everson case as an opportunity to explain the court's decision to rewrite American history. It wasn't pretty.

In a 5–4 decision, the court sided with New Jersey and upheld the state law, but Black's opinion contained a long dissertation on the history and meaning of religious freedom in America. In what has become a common misconception of early American history, Black argued that "a large proportion of the early settlers of this country came here from Europe to escape the bondage of laws which compelled them to support and attend government-favored churches."[20] This may have been true for the Quakers of Pennsylvania or the Pilgrims of Massachusetts (at least in part), but virtually every one of the original thirteen British North American colonies maintained a state-established church. The Orthodox Anglicans dominated Virginia and the Carolinas; the Puritan Church was supreme (and mandatory) in New England. Rhode Island and Pennsylvania offered refuge for religious dissenters, but they were the exception, not the rule. Georgia prohibited Catholics from living there, and Maryland, once founded as a colony for Catholic Englishmen, barred Catholics from voting. It seems Black was reading history in reverse, and even he recognized that much of American colonial history was dotted with taxpayer-supported denominations.

Black rectified the problem by bringing the ghosts of Thomas Jefferson and James Madison into town on a white horse carrying the banner of religious freedom. Jefferson drafted the Virginia Statute for Religious Freedom in 1777 and Madison presented it to the Virginia General Assembly in 1779. The statute disestablished the Church of England and offered religious liberty for all Christians and Jews; however, it took seven years for the statute to become law because it was fervently opposed by the majority of the people of Virginia. But Black used both Jefferson and Madison's advocacy for "religious freedom" as a springboard for his views on incorporation. Black argued that Madison, as the "Father of the Bill of Rights" and "Father of the Constitution," really intended the First Amendment to mirror the Virginia Statute, and that Jefferson's famous (or infamous) 1802 letter to the Connecticut Danbury Baptists where he penned that he believed there must be "a wall of separation between church and state" conclusively proved that the First Amendment applied to the states. This was disingenuous at best.

The Virginia Statute only applied to *Virginia*, hence the introduction of the bill in the Virginia General Assembly, and Jefferson's letter to the

Danbury Baptists is often taken out of context. Black, perhaps purposely, fell into this trap. In 1801 the leaders of the Danbury Baptists penned Jefferson a letter of congratulation on his election as president. The Baptists wrote that, "Sir, we are sensible that the president of the United States is not the national legislator, *and also sensible that the national government cannot destroy the laws of each state*; but our hopes are strong that the sentiments of our beloved president, which have had such genial effect already, like the radiant beams of the sun, will shine and prevail through all these states and all the world, till hierarchy and tyranny be destroyed from the earth"[emphasis added].[21] Jefferson responded that he hoped the precedent established by the ratification of the First Amendment would "tend to restore to man all his natural rights, convinced he has no natural right in opposition to his social duties," and he assured them that the general government would not interfere in their freedom of conscience.[22] The Danbury Baptists realized the First Amendment did not apply to the states, and Jefferson agreed, though he hoped the spirit of religious freedom would in time prevail in every state. Black also ignored the history of the framing and ratification of the First Amendment, the rejection of Madison's "incorporation amendment" by the First Congress, and the several decisions against applying the Bill of Rights against the states beginning with *Barron v. Baltimore* in 1833. This was hardly the concrete support Black needed for incorporation, but he ran with it.

Black issued perhaps his most infamous decision in the *Engel v. Vitale* case of 1962. The state of New York urged public schools to craft morning prayers for those students willing to participate. This was not unusual. American public schools had since their inception mandated daily Bible readings and public prayer, but some American Protestants had worried about the potential for Catholics to hijack morning services. The "Know Nothing" Party of the 1850s advocated a religious test for public school teachers and insisted that only the King James Bible be used in daily Bible readings. In some locations, even in the 1850s, Catholics were denied the right to vote. Nevertheless, religion in public schools was an accepted practice for most of America's history, that is until Hugo Black jotted his majority opinion in *Engel v. Vitale* in 1962.

Predictably, Black found that, "By using its public school system to encourage recitation of the Regents' prayer, the State of New York has adopted a practice wholly inconsistent with the Establishment Clause [of the First Amendment]." He proceeded to defend this position by doubling down and restating his imaginary history of the First Amendment and the founding period. Black again ignored every kernel of American history that refuted his incorporationist fairy tale, and used that same fantasy to deny that his decision would destroy religion in America:

> And there were men of this same faith in the power of prayer who led the fight for adoption of our Constitution and also for our Bill of Rights with the very guarantees of religious freedom that forbid the sort of governmental activity which New York has attempted here. These men knew that the First Amendment, which tried to put an end to governmental control of religion and of prayer, was not written to destroy either. They knew, rather, that it was written to quiet well justified fears which nearly all of them felt arising out of an awareness that governments of the past had shackled men's tongues to make them speak only the religious thoughts that government wanted them to speak and to pray only to the God that government wanted them to pray to. It is neither sacrilegious nor anti-religious to say that each separate government in this country should stay out of the business of writing or sanctioning official prayers and leave that purely religious function to the people themselves and to those the people choose to look to for religious guidance.[23]

Black may have believed this, but the net result of his decision was the exact thing he swore would not happen. Even offering a "moment of silence" before any school activity today can be challenged in federal court as a public display of religion. Contrary to what Black wrote, this is not what the founding generation had in mind when they ratified the First Amendment.

In time, Black's interpretation of the First Amendment and incorporation became the standard by which all legislation, both state and federal, was measured. State laws against pornography were struck down by the Supreme Court with Black in the majority. "Indecent" images fell under the purview of "free press" and because Black had disingenuously reasoned that the Fourteenth Amendment applied to the states, no state could clean up its own backyard. So-called Miranda rights were the byproduct of a five-judge majority in the 1966 case of *Miranda v. Arizona,* a majority who considered it a violation of the Bill of Rights if criminals were not informed of their "legal rights" at the time of their arrest. Fourth Amendment rights incorporated through the Due Process clause of the Fourteenth Amendment placed American taxpayers on the hook for police errors and later legalized abortion. "No law means no law," Black often thundered. Even after Black died, the court continued to follow his lead in a host of cases that the founding generation would have considered to be purely state issues. For example, the Supreme Court struck down state execution laws as a violation of the Eighth Amendment and eventually incorporated virtually every one of the first eight amendments of the Bill of Rights. The last to fall for political reasons was the Second Amendment, but now even that has been incorporated through a disingenuous reading of the Fourteenth Amendment.

Why was Black so interested in incorporation of the First Amendment and later the first eight amendments to the Bill of Rights? His support for the Klan in the 1920s might provide some clues. The Klan became one of the leading voices for a "wall of separation" in the progressive era. Their disdain for Catholics led them to zealously agitate for a national solution to "popery" and "immorality" in America. What they wanted was an all-white, Protestant America through national legislation, meaning the prohibition of any law, federal or state, that allowed Catholics to gain a foothold into American society. Black's eager defense of his Methodist minister friend as solicitor in Jefferson County and his humble appreciation for Klan support in his bid for the United States Senate in 1926 highlighted a political and legal career in which the voice of the Klan often whispered in his ear. His written decisions on the Supreme Court were the culmination of his belief that the only way to hamper Catholics was through the power of the federal court system and incorporation. Decisions in other areas were simply the icing on the cake.

Both modern progressives and civil libertarians often regard Black's misinterpretation of the Fourteenth Amendment to be a triumph of liberty over tyranny, particularly when it suits their political agenda. But this comes at a cost. Federalism, the cornerstone of the American political experiment, has been lost, not by constitutional amendment, but through the whimsical historical fantasies of several Supreme Court justices, Hugo Black foremost among them. Most Americans today look for the national government to offer national solutions to every pressing political issue, particularly when they believe their First or Fourth or Second Amendment "rights" have been violated by one level of government or another. Hamilton's nationalist dream could not have been complete without the federal court system, and Black drove the final nail into the coffin of the original Constitution.

CHAPTER THIRTEEN

THINK LOCALLY, ACT LOCALLY

lexander Hamilton and his acolytes did more damage to the American government than any other group in the history of the United States. "Nationalism" turned the founding on its head and created conflict where none existed. Contrary to what most Americans have been taught in school, states' rights, once the cornerstone of the American federal union, *prevented* conflict. Once every issue became national in scope, Americans lost the ability or the desire to directly confront problems that were considered local issues for much of American history. Americans whine about education and look for the president or the Congress to "solve" that issue. The same holds true for crime, healthcare, marriage, gun ownership, the environment, or a host of other matters that most of the members of the founding generation considered to be off-limits for the general Congress.

Americans are angry, and after every election half of the population feels alienated. There are clear winners and losers in a "national" plebiscite. The bare majority will spend the next four to eight years rolling out a "national" plan of government that the other half of the population will hate. The winners gloat and the losers pout, uncertain about their future in an America they don't recognize.

But that is not how the Constitution was designed. What if it didn't matter who won the presidential election, or which party controlled Congress, or how the Supreme Court ruled on a particular issue? If we adopted a more Jeffersonian approach to American government that would certainly be the case. Men like Spencer Roane, Abel Upshur, Philip Barbour, John Taylor of Caroline, St. George Tucker, and Thomas Ritchie offered an alternative to the nationalist approach to American government. This Virginia school focused on decentralization as a way to protect political minorities from abuse at the hands of the majority. If we adhered to a central government led by Virginia and not New York, one of Jefferson and not Hamilton, Americans would be less concerned about who led Congress and more concerned about who occupied their statehouses.

This would not only be the correct way to interpret the original Constitution, it would produce a happier population. America is too big, its population too vast, and its political representation too limited to have the national government in Washington, DC make decisions that should be left to the people of the states. Our representative ratio in Congress, once pegged by George Washington at 30,000:1 now stands at a whopping 735,000:1 and growing! Washington said that the original ratio of 40,000:1 was too large for a representative government. What would he think about 735,000:1? The fact is we have lost the ability to control the government in Washington, DC. The Jeffersonians could see the writing on the wall in the early federal period. "National" power could be more dangerous to liberty and the stability of the federal republic than decentralization.

California, Washington, and Oregon have openly spoken of secession following Donald Trump's election. The same thing happened in 2008 when Barack Obama was elected president, only then it was the South and the Mountain West that led the charge. This is a symptom of the disease of Hamilton's America. Americans don't want to be governed by a foreign people, and what most people realize, though they won't admit it, is that the "one people" theory pushed by every nationalist from Hamilton forward is not only historically inaccurate, it is detrimental to the political welfare of the constituent parts of the union. Why should Californians be subjected to the laws of Alabama or vice-versa? At the heart of each of these secession "movements" is a realization that local communities are better equipped to handle the social and cultural issues of the day. It has always been so.

Wouldn't it be more responsible for the local school board to make decisions for the people of the state or for the people of the community to have a government and society that better reflects their social and moral values? Think locally, act locally should be the political slogan of the twenty-first century. Hamilton's America, the "one nation indivisible" beaten into our heads since we were five, would work well for a homogenous population, but Americans have never—never—enjoyed that. From the colonial period to the present, Americans have been a diverse lot. Cavalier Virginians and Puritan Massachusettians never saw eye to eye on government policy. They in fact hated each other, but a union with very limited power in the central authority allowed each people to develop their political community as they saw fit. It would be immoral for one group of people to tell another how to live, yet this type of cultural imperialism is foisted upon Americans, both left and right, on a daily basis in Hamilton's American "nation."

We live in Hamilton's America, but if we want an America that reflects who we are and have been as a people, Hamilton's America needs to be buried next to the bastard from Nevis. The only way to "make America great again" is to rid the people of the states of Hamilton's curse and take government into our own hands at the state and local level. Maybe then, Hamilton, Marshall, Story, and Black could cease screwing up the original federal republic.

NOTES

INTRODUCTION

1. Liam Deacon, "Anti-Brexit Bob Geldof: I Led the Booing of Mike Pence at Hamilton," December 3, 2016, Breitbart.com, http://www.breitbart.com/london/2016/12/03/anti-brexit-bob-geldof-led-booing-mike-pence-hamilton/.
2. Christopher Mele and Patrick Healy, "'Hamilton' Had Some Unscripted Lines for Pence. Trump Wasn't Happy," November 19, 2016, *New York Times*, http://www.nytimes.com/2016/11/19/us/mike-pence-hamilton.html.
3. Alissa Wilkinson, "The Hamilton Mixtape feels like the original album that Hamilton was always covering," December 8, 2016, Vox.com, http://www.vox.com/culture/2016/12/6/13843722/hamilton-mixtape-lin-manuel-miranda.
4. Brion McClanahan, *The Politically Incorrect Guide to the Founding Fathers* (Washington DC: Regnery, 2009).
5. *National Federation of Independent Business v. Sebelius*, 567 U.S. ___ (2012), 183 L. Ed. 2d 450, 132 S.Ct. 2566.

CHAPTER 1: HAMILTON VS. HAMILTON

1. Russell Kirk, *The Conservative Mind: From Burke to Elliot* (Washington, DC: Regnery, 1953); Forrest McDonald, *Alexander Hamilton: A Biography* (New York: W.W. Norton & Company, 1979).

2.   George Will, *Restoration: Congress, Term Limits and the Recovery of Deliberative Democracy* (New York: The Free Press, 1992), 167.

3.   David Brooks and William Kristol, "What Ails Conservatism?" *Wall Street Journal*, September 15, 1997.

4.   Richard Brookhiser, *Alexander Hamilton: American* (New York: Free Press, 1999).

5.   Michael Lind, *Hamilton's Republic: Readings in the American Democratic Nationalist Tradition* (New York: Free Press, 1997).

6.   Stephen Knott, *Alexander Hamilton and the Persistence of Myth* (Lawrence, KS: University Press of Kansas, 2002).

7.   "Thomas Jefferson to Benjamin Rush, 16 January 1811," *Founders Online*, National Archives, last modified July 12, 2016, http://founders.archives.gov/documents/Jefferson/03-03-02-0231. Original source: *The Papers of Thomas Jefferson*, Retirement Series, vol. 3, *12 August 1810 to 17 June 1811*, ed. J. Jefferson Looney. Princeton: Princeton University Press, 2006, 304–308.

CHAPTER 2: FROM PHILADELPHIA TO POUGHKEEPSIE

1.   John P. Kaminski, et al., eds., *The Documentary History of the Ratification of the Constitution* (Madison, WI: State Historical Society of Wisconsin, 1981-2016), XIII: 476.

2.   Jonathan Elliot, ed., *The Debates in the Several State Conventions on the Adoption of the Federal Constitution as Recommended by the General Convention at Philadelphia in 1787* (New York: Burt Franklin Reprints, 1974), II: 224, 334, 250.

3.   Ibid., V: 193.

4.   Forrest McDonald, *Alexander Hamilton: A Biography* (New York: W. W. Norton & Company, 1982), 105; Max Farrand, ed., *The Records of the Federal Convention of 1787* (New Haven: Yale University Press, 1966), I: 363.

5.   Elliot, *The Debates in the Several State Conventions,* V: 199-206.

6.   Kaminski et al. eds., *The Documentary History of the Ratification of the Constitution*, XV: 217, 222.

7.   Elliot, *The Debates in the Several State Conventions*, II: 353, 356.

8.   Ibid., 362, 370–71.

9.   Kaminski, *The Documentary History of the Ratification of the Constitution*, XXII: 1998–2002.

10.   Ibid., 2004-2013.

11.   Ibid., 2011.

12.   Farrand, *The Records of the Federal Convention of 1787*, I: 297–98.

CHAPTER 3: ASSUMPTION AND IMPLIED POWERS

1.   *Annals of Congress*, 1st Congress, 1st Session, 393–94.

2.   Ibid., 408.

3.   Ibid., 616.

4.   Ibid.

5.   Ibid., 631.
6.   Lance Banning, ed., *Liberty and Order: The First American Party Struggle* (Indianapolis, IN: Liberty Fund, Inc., 2004), 76.
7.   Ibid., 76–83.
8.   For a concise analysis of James Jackson's impact on American conservatism, see Brion McClanahan and Clyde Wilson, *Forgotten Conservatives in American History* (Greta, LA: Pelican Publishing, 2012), 17–23.
9.   *Annals of Congress,*, 1st Congress, 2nd Session, 1132, 1182.
10. Ibid., 1396.
11. Ibid., 1392.
12. Ibid., 1409-10.
13. Ibid., 1542.
14. Ibid., 1544.
15. Ibid., 1590–91.
16. Farrand, *The Records of the Federal Convention of 1787*, II: 6, 322, 327, 328, 352, 355, 368, 377.
17. Ibid., III: 366.

CHAPTER 4: THE BANK

1.   Worthington C. Ford, ed. et. al., *Journals of the Continental Congress 1774-1789* (Washington D.C., 1904-37), XX: 545; XXI: 1185.
2.   See Janet Wilson, "The Bank of North America and Pennsylvania Politics: 1781–1787," *The Pennsylvania Magazine of History and Biography* 66 no. 1 (January 1942): 3-28.
3.   Mark David Hall and Kermit L. Hall, eds., *The Collected Works of James Wilson* (Indianapolis, IN: Liberty Fund, 2007), I: 64–69.
4.   Farrand, ed., *Records of the Federal Convention*, II: 529–530.
5.   Ibid., II: 615-616.
6.   *Annals of Congress*, 1st Congress, 2nd Session, 1945–46.
7.   Elliot, ed., *Debates in the Several State Conventions*, III: 443.
8.   Kaminski, et. al., eds., *The Documentary History of the Ratification of the Constitution*, XV: 220.
9.   Paul Leicester Ford, ed., *The Federalist : A commentary on the Constitution of the United States by Alexander Hamilton, James Madison and John Jay edited with notes, illustrative documents and a copious index* (New York : Henry Holt and Company, 1898), 655.
10. Ibid., 655–676.

CHAPTER 5: THE REBELLION

1.   Thomas P. Slaughter, *The Whiskey Rebellion: Frontier Epilogue to the American Revolution* (New York: Oxford University Press, 1986), 95–96.
2.   "Final Version of the Second Report on the Further Provision Necessary for Establishing Public Credit (Report on a National Bank), 13 December 1790,"

Founders Online, National Archives, last modified July 12, 2016, http://founders. archives.gov/documents/Hamilton/01-07-02-0229-0003. Original source: Harold C. Syrett, ed., *The Papers of Alexander Hamilton,* vol. 7, *September 1790–January 1791* (New York: Columbia University Press, 1963), 305–342.

3.   Henry Cabot Lodge, ed., *The Federalist: A Commentary on the Constitution of the United States Being a Collection of Essays Written in Support of the Constitution Agreed Upon September 17, 1787 by The Federal Convention* (New York: G.P. Putnam's Sons, 1888), 67–72.

4.   Quoted in Slaughter, *The Whiskey Rebellion,* 98.

5.   *Annals of Congress,* 1st Congress, 2nd Session, 1891–92.

6.   See William Findley, *History of the Insurrection of the Four Western Counties of Pennsylvania in the Year 1794* (Philadelphia: Samuel Harrison Smith, 1796); Slaughter, *The Whiskey Rebellion,* 109–116.

7.   Slaughter, *The Whiskey Rebellion,* 117–118.

8.   "To Alexander Hamilton from George Washington, 31 August 1792," *Founders Online,* National Archives, last modified July 12, 2016, http://founders.archives. gov/documents/Hamilton/01-12-02-0236. Original source: Syrett, *The Papers of Alexander Hamilton,* vol. 12, *July 1792–October 1792,* 304–305.

9.   "To Alexander Hamilton from Edmund Randolph, 8 September 1792," *Founders Online,* National Archives, last modified July 12, 2016, http://founders.archives. gov/documents/Hamilton/01-12-02-0261. Original source: Syrett, *The Papers of Alexander Hamilton,* vol. 12, *July 1792–October 1792,* 336–340.

10.   Slaughter, *The Whiskey Rebellion,* 119–120.

11.   Forrest, McDonald, *Alexander Hamilton: A* Biography (New York: W. W. Norton, 1982) 255–257.

12.   "To George Washington from Alexander Hamilton, 11 September 1792," *Founders Online,* National Archives, last modified July 12, 2016, http://founders.archives. gov/documents/Washington/05-11-02-0051. Original source: Christine Sternberg Patrick ed., *The Papers of George Washington,* Presidential Series, vol. 11, *16 August 1792–15 January 1793* (Charlottesville: University of Virginia Press, 2002), 108–110.

13.   "From George Washington to Thomas Jefferson, 15 September 1792," *Founders Online,* National Archives, last modified July 12, 2016, http://founders.archives. gov/documents/Washington/05-11-02-0055. Original source: Sternberg Patrick, *The Papers of George Washington,* 113–115.

14.   George Washington: "Proclamation 3B—Cessation of Violence and Obstruction of Justice in Protest of Liquor Laws," September 15, 1792. Online by Gerhard Peters and John T. Woolley, *The American Presidency Project,* http://www.presidency. ucsb.edu/ws/?pid=65427.

15.   "From George Washington to Alexander Hamilton, 17 September 1792," *Founders Online,* National Archives, last modified July 12, 2016, http://founders.archives. gov/documents/Washington/05-11-02-0061. Original source: Sternberg Patrick,

The Papers of George Washington, Presidential Series, vol. 11, *16 August 1792–15 January 1793*, 126–127.

16. Ron Chernow, *Alexander Hamilton* (New York: Penguin Books, 2005), 470; Slaughter, *The Whiskey Rebellion*, 179–180.

17. "Conference Concerning the Insurrection in Western Pennsylvania, [2 August 1794]," *Founders Online*, National Archives, last modified July 12, 2016, http://founders.archives.gov/documents/Hamilton/01-17-02-0009. Original source: Syrett, *The Papers of Alexander Hamilton*, vol. 17, *August 1794–December 1794*, 9–14.

18. Ibid.; Chernow, *Alexander Hamilton*, 476.

19. "Tully No. III, [28 August 1794]," *Founders Online*, National Archives, last modified July 12, 2016, http://founders.archives.gov/documents/Hamilton/01-17-02-0130. Original source: Syrett, *The Papers of Alexander Hamilton*, vol. 17, *August 1794–December 1794*, 159–161.

20. *Annals of Congress*, House of Representatives, 2nd Congress, 1st Session, 556–58, 576–77.

CHAPTER 6: THE PROCLAMATION

1. Elliot, ed., *Debates in the Several State Conventions*, V: 203–205.

2. "Conversation with George Beckwith, [October 1789]," Founders Online, National Archives, last modified July 12, 2016, http://founders.archives.gov/documents/Hamilton/01-05-02-0273. Original source: Syrett ed., *The Papers of Alexander Hamilton, vol. 5, June 1788–November 1789*, 482–490.

3. The best singular study on this issue is Julian P. Boyd, *Number 7: Alexander Hamilton's Secret Attempts to Control American Foreign Policy* (Princeton: Princeton University Press, 1964).

4. Harry Ammon, *The Genet Mission* (New York: Norton & Co., 1973), 44–45.

5. "From Alexander Hamilton to George Washington, 5 April 1793," Founders Online, National Archives, last modified July 12, 2016, http://founders.archives.gov/documents/Hamilton/01-14-02-0181. Original source: Syrett, *The Papers of Alexander Hamilton, vol. 14, February 1793–June 1793*, 291–292.

6. Morton J. Frisch ed., *The Pacificus-Helvidius Debates of 1793-1794: Toward the Completion of the American Founding* (Indianapolis: Liberty Fund, Inc., 2007), 1.

7. "Defense of the President's Neutrality Proclamation, [May 1793]," Founders Online, National Archives, last modified July 12, 2016, http://founders.archives.gov/documents/Hamilton/01-14-02-0340. Original source: Syrett, *The Papers of Alexander Hamilton, vol. 14, February 1793–June 1793*, 502–507.

8. Frisch, *The Pacificus-Helvidius Debates*, 8–17.

9. "To James Madison from Thomas Jefferson, 7 July 1793," Founders Online, National Archives, last modified July 12, 2016, http://founders.archives.gov/documents/Madison/01-15-02-0037. Original source: Thomas A. Mason, Robert

A. Rutland, and Jeanne K. Sisson, *The Papers of James Madison, vol. 15, 24 March 1793–20 April 1795* (Charlottesville: University Press of Virginia, 1985), 43.

10.   Frisch, *The Pacificus-Helvidius Debates*, 55–64.

CHAPTER 7: MARSHALL VS. MARSHALL

1.   Sam J. Ervin, Jr., *Humor of a Country Lawyer* (Chapel Hill: University of North Carolina Press, 1983), 38.

2.   Leonard Baker, *John Marshall: A Life in Law* (New York: Macmillan, 1974), 312.

3.   John Marshall, *An Autobiographical Sketch by John Marshall* (Ann Arbor, MI: University of Michigan Press, 1937), 23.

4.   "To Alexander Hamilton from John Marshall, 1 January 1801," *Founders Online*, National Archives, last modified July 12, 2016, http://founders.archives.gov/documents/Hamilton/01-25-02-0154. Original source: Syrett ed., *The Papers of Alexander Hamilton*, vol. 25, *July 1800–April 1802*, 290–292.

5.   Elliot, ed., *Debates in the Several State Conventions*, III: 551–562.

CHAPTER 8: JUDICIAL REVIEW AND CONTRACTS

1.   *Marbury v. Madison*, 5 U.S. 1 Cranch 137–180 (1803).

2.   "From Thomas Jefferson to Abigail Smith Adams, 11 September 1804," Founders Online, National Archives, last modified July 12, 2016, http://founders.archives.gov/documents/Adams/99-03-02-1317.

3.   Leonard Baker, *John Marshall: A Life in Law* (New York: Macmillan, 1974), 409.

4.   Ibid., 411.

5.   Farrand, ed., *Records of the Federal Convention*, I: 97–101; Elliot, ed., *Debates in the Several State Conventions*, V: 429, 483.

6.   "From Thomas Jefferson to Abigail Smith Adams, 11 September 1804," Founders Online, National Archives, last modified July 12, 2016, http://founders.archives.gov/documents/Adams/99-03-02-1317; "From Thomas Jefferson to William Johnson, 12 June 1823," Founders Online, National Archives, last modified July 12, 2016, http://founders.archives.gov/documents/Jefferson/98-01-02-3562.

7.   Elliot, *Debates in the Several State Conventions*, V: 430.

8.   Ibid., II: 489.

9.   Ibid., 196.

10.   Ibid., VI: 156–57.

11.   Ibid., V: 468.

12.   Benjamin F. Wrigt, *The Contract Clause of the Constitution* (Cambridge: Harvard University Press, 1938), 95.

13.   *Fletcher v. Peck*, 10 U.S. 6 Cranch 87 (1810).

14.   John E. Hall, ed., *The American Law Journal* (Baltimore: Edward Coale, et. al., 1814) V: 455.

CHAPTER 9: MARSHALL CODIFIES IMPLIED POWERS

1. *Annals of Congress*, Senate, 11th Congress, 3rd Session, 346.
2. James D. Richardson, *Messages and Papers of the Presidents* (Washington, DC: Government Printing Office, 1897), II: 540.
3. James Madison, "Seventh Annual Message," December 5, 1815. Online by Gerhard Peters and John T. Woolley, The American Presidency Project, http://www. presidency.ucsb.edu/ws/?pid=29457.
4. Kevin R. C. Gutzman, *James Madison and the Making of America* (New York: St. Martin's Press, 2012), 330–31.
5. For a concise history of the Panic of 1819, see Murry N. Rothbard, *The Panic of 1819: Reactions and Policies* (New York: Columbia University Press, 1962).
6. Richard E. Ellis, *Aggressive Nationalism: McCulloch v. Maryland and the Foundation of Federal Authority in the Young Republic* (New York: Oxford University Press, 2007), 67–76.
7. *McCulloch v. Maryland* (1819), 4 Wheaton, 323–330.
8. Ibid., 375–76.
9. All quotes from the Marshall opinion can be found in Ibid.,400–437.
10. Quoted in Gutzman, *James Madison*, 351.
11. *Richmond Enquirer*, March 30, 1819.
12. Ibid., June 22, 1819.
13. John Taylor of Caroline, *Construction Construed and Constitutions Vindicated* (Richmond: Shepherd & Pollard, 1820), i–ii.
14. Ibid., 42–43.
15. Ibid., 165–66.

CHAPTER 10: THE MARSHALL COURT AND THE STATES

1. Journal of William Maclay, United States Senator from Pennsylvania 1789–1791, 88, 118.
2. Annals of Congress, 1st Congress, 1st Session, 814.
3. Ibid., 829.
4. John P. Kaminski et al. eds., *The Documentary History of the Ratification of the Constitution* (Charlottesville: The University of Virginia Press, 2009), III: 352, 490.
5. Ibid., 553.
6. Quoted in James McClellan, *Joseph Story and the American Constitution: A Study in Political and Legal Thought* (Norman: University of Oklahoma Press, 1971), 243.
7. Quoted in Leonard Baker, *A Life in Law: John Marshall* (New York: Macmillan, 1974), 576.
8. 1 Wheaton (1816), 314–15.
9. Ibid., 320–21.
10. Albert J. Beveridge, *The Life of John Marshall* (Boston: Houghton, Mifflin, Co. 1919), IV: 82–83.

11. 1 Wheaton (1816), 341–51.

12. Quoted inMcClellan, *Joseph Story and the American Constitution*, 246.

13. William S. Belko, *Philip Pendleton Barbour in Jacksonian America: An Old Republican in King Andrew's Court* (Tuscaloosa, AL: University of Alabama Press, 2016), 77–78.

14. 6 Wheaton (1821), 290-300.

15. Ibid., 319–323.

16. Ibid., 344, 347.

17. Ibid., 353–54, 375.

18. "Virginia Opposition to Chief Justice Marshall," John P. Branch Historical Papers of Randolph-Macon College 2 (1906): 78–183.

19. "To James Madison from Spencer Roane, 17 April 1821," Founders Online, National Archives, last modified October 5, 2016, http://founders.archives.gov/documents/Madison/04-02-02-0252. Original source: David B. Mattern et al. eds., *The Papers of James Madison, Retirement Series, vol. 2, 1 February 1820–26 February 1823* (Charlottesville: University of Virginia Press, 2013), 302–303.

CHAPTER 11: JOSEPH STORY AND THE *COMMENTARIES*

1. William Wetmore Story, *Life and Letters of Joseph Story* (London: John Chapman, 1851), 277.

2. Joseph Story, *Commentaries on the Constitution of the United States with a Preliminary Review of the Constitutional History of the Colonies and the States, Before the Adoption of the Constitution* (Boston: Hilliard, Gray, and Co., 1833), I: vi.

3. Ibid., 164.

4. Ibid., 186.

5. Ibid., 191, 194–95.

6. Ibid., 197–98, 203.

7. "From James Madison to Thomas Ritchie, 15 September 1821," Founders Online, National Archives, last modified October 5, 2016, http://founders.archives.gov/documents/Madison/04-02-02-0321. Original source: David B. Mattern et al. eds., *The Papers of James Madison, Retirement Series, vol. 2, 1 February 1820–26 February 1823*, (Charlottesville: University of Virginia Press, 2013), 381–82.

8. Clyde N. Wilson, ed., *View of the Constitution of the United States with Selected Writings* (Indianapolis: Liberty Fund, Inc., 1999), 91.

9. Story, *Commentaries on the Constitution of the United States*, I: 289.

10. Ibid., 319.

11. See Brion McClanahan, *The Founding Fathers Guide to the Constitution* (Washington, DC: Regnery History, 2012), 7–13.

12. Story, *Commentaries on the Constitution of the United States*, I: 343.

13. Ibid., 406–07; 418.

14. Ibid., 421.

15.   Ibid., 424.
16.   Ibid., 437.
17.   Ibid., 441.
18.   Ibid., 445.
19.   Ibid., 446.
20.   Ibid., III: 427.
21.   R. Kent Newmyer, *Supreme Court Justice Joseph Story: Statesman of the Old Republic* (Chapel Hill: University of North Carolina Press, 1985), 185.
22.   John Taylor, *New Views of the Constitution of the United States* (Washington, DC: Way and Gideon, 1823), 6.
23.   Ibid., 7.
24.   Ibid.
25.   Ibid., 172.
26.   Ibid., 11.
27.   Abel P. Upshur, *A Brief Enquiry into the Nature and Character of Our Federal Government: Being a Review of Judge Story's Commentaries on the Constitution of the United States* (Philadelphia: John Campbell, 1863), 18.
28.   Ibid., 17.
29.   Ibid., 15–16.
30.   Ibid., 23.
31.   Ibid., 78.
32.   Ibid., 85.
33.   Ibid., 131.
34.   Ibid., 126–27.

CHAPTER 12: HUGO BLACK AND INCORPORATION

1.   The best volumes on the misunderstanding of the Fourteenth Amendment are Raoul Berger, *Government by Judiciary: The Transformation of the Fourteenth Amendment* (Cambridge: Harvard University Press, 1977); Charles Fairman, "Does the Fourteenth Amendment Incorporate the Bill of Rights? The Original Understanding." *Stanford Law Review* 2, no. 1 (1949): 5-139. doi:10.2307/1226431; Stanley Morrison, "Does the Fourteenth Amendment Incorporate the Bill of Rights? The Judicial Interpretation." *Stanford Law Review*, vol. 2, no. 1, 1949, pp. 140–173. doi:10.2307/1226432..
2.   Annals of Congress, 1st Congress, 1st Session, 452.
3.   Ibid., 782–83.
4.   7 Peters 247–250.
5.   Roger K. Newman, *Hugo Black: A Biography* (New York: Fordham University Press, 1997), 3.
6.   Michael A. Ross, *Justice of Shattered Dreams: Samuel Francis Miller and the Supreme Court During the Civil War Era* (Baton Rouge, LA: Louisiana State University Press, 2003), 79.

7. All quotes from Miller's decision are taken from Stephen K. Williams, ed., *Cases Argued and Decided in the Supreme Court of the United States* (New York: The Lawyers Cooperative Publishing Company, 1884), XXI: 402–410.

8. Benj. B. Kendrick, *The Journal of the Joint Committee of Fifteen on Reconstruction: 89th Congress 1865-67* (Ph.D. Dissertation, Columbia University, 1914), 46.

9. Congressional Globe, 39th Congress, 1st Session, 1064.

10. Ibid., 1077.

11. Ibid., 1270.

12. Ibid., 1034.

13. Ibid., 1088.

14. Ibid., 2764-65.

15. Ibid., 2961.

16. Ibid., 1294.

17. Ibid., 1089–1090, 1093.

18. *Adamson v. California* 332 U.S. 69–92 (1947).

19. *Cantwell v. Connecticut*, 310 U.S. 296 (1940); For an excellent review of the history of incorporation of the First Amendment, see Thomas E. Woods and Kevin R.C. Gutzman, *Who Killed the Constitution? The Federal Government vs. American Liberty from World War I to Barack Obama* (New York: Three Rivers Press, 2008), 103–117.

20. *Everson v. Board of Education*, 330 U.S. 1 (1947).

21. "To Thomas Jefferson from the Danbury Baptist Association, [after 7 October 1801]," Founders Online, National Archives, last modified October 5, 2016, http://founders.archives.gov/documents/Jefferson/01-35-02-0331. Original source: Barbara B. Oberg ed., *The Papers of Thomas Jefferson, vol. 35, 1 August–30 November 1801*, (Princeton: Princeton University Press, 2008), 407–409.

22. "To the Danbury Baptist Association, 1 January 1802," Founders Online, National Archives, last modified October 5, 2016, http://founders.archives.gov/documents/Jefferson/01-36-02-0152-0006. Original source: Oberg, *The Papers of Thomas Jefferson, vol. 36, 1 December 1801–3 March 1802* (Princeton: Princeton University Press, 2009), 258.

23. *Engel v. Vitale*, 370 U.S. 421 (1962).

INDEX

201